Christian Philosophy and Its Future

Six Essays

Christian Philosophy and Its Future

Gerard Smith, S.J.

Marquette University Press
1971

BR
100
.S53

Copyright 1971

Gerard Smith, S.J.

LIBRARY OF CONGRESS CATALOG NUMBER: 75-140071

SBN 87462-439-8

Contents

Editor's Foreword .... *vii*

Foreword: "Metaphysics Made Gay, Not Clear" .... *ix*

Editor's Preface .... *xi*

   I. Philosophy and the Knowledges of Man
      What Is Philosophy About? 3

 II. Philosophy and Theology
     Mr. Adler and the Order of Learning 27
     *The Position of Philosophy
         in a Catholic College* 51

III. An Instance of Christian Philosophy
     *Philosophy and the Unity
         of Man's Ultimate End* 79

IV. The Future of Christian Philosophy
     A Note on the Future of Catholic Philosophy 99
     An Appraisal of Scholastic Philosophy 111

Editor's Foreword

The editor gratefully acknowledges her indebtedness to the following:

To The American Catholic Philosophical Association, for permission to reprint three articles by Father Gerard Smith, S.J.; these articles originally appeared in the *Proceedings of the American Catholic Philosophical Association*:

"Philosophy and the Unity of Man's Ultimate End"
(Vol. XXVII, 1953, pp. 60-83)
"The Position of Philosophy in a Catholic College"
(Vol. XXIX, 1955, pp. 20-40)
"An Appraisal of Scholastic Philosophy"
(Vol. XL, 1966, pp. 41-54)

To The National Catholic Educational Association, Suite 350, One Dupont Circle, Washington, D.C. 20036, for permission to reprint Father Smith's article, "Mr. Adler and the Order of Learning," which originally appeared in the *NCEA Bulletin* (Vol. XXXIX, August, 1942, pp. 140-162).

To Aubier, publisher in Paris, France, for permission to print an English translation of Father Smith's French article, "Note sur L'Avenir de la Philosophie Catholique," which appeared in *L'Homme devant Dieu: Mélanges offerts au Père Henri de Lubac*, Vol. III (1963), pp. 277-285.

To Dr. Paul M. Byrne, Chairman of the Department of Philosophy, Marquette University, for his encouragement of this project.

To Mr. Clifford L. Helbert, Dean of the College of Journalism, Marquette University, for designing this book.

The Foreword

A Christian Philosopher Speaks on the Text of *De Veritate*, q. 21, a. 5, ad 8: "The existence of a thing is called a being, not because it has some existence other than itself, but because by that existence the *thing* is said to be."

METAPHYSICS MADE GAY, NOT CLEAR

by Gerard Smith, S.J.

A student once thought a thing's "being"
Couldn't have any possible meaning,
'Til he got this great light,
And was filled with delight:
A honey bee's being is bee-ing.

Yet, he reasoned, if bee-ing *is* being,
And it's clear there are beings *not* bee-ing,
There's this left to see,
That simply "to-be"
Is the nature of being as being.

Come heavenly Muse—now, *that* being
Simply can't be a honey bee's bee-ing,
For then there would be
No thing but a bee!
Then what about *me*? *I'm* not bee-ing!

To account, then, for bee-ing and me-ing
I must see there's a *cause* of each ing-ing,
And if this is so,
I'm all set to know
An "ing" that's not me-ing or bee-ing.

His dictis, since God is just Ing,
Not me or *any* old thing—
Well, thank God for *that,*
I'm under my hat,
And can talk to Him, pray, yes, and sing.

Editor's Preface

The nature of Christian philosophy is a subject that has interested Father Smith for many years. He studied theology at Ore Place, Hastings, England, and at Fourvière, Lyons, France, before being ordained as a Jesuit priest in Dublin, Ireland, in 1927. He was head of the Religion Department at Marquette University, 1929-1930. He studied philosophy at the Pontifical Institute of Mediaeval Studies at the University of Toronto where he received his Ph.D. in 1936. He taught philosophy at St. Louis University and at Marquette University. He served as chairman of the Department of Philosophy at Marquette University for twenty-two years (1944-1966).

Throughout these years he has frequently thought about such questions as: What is philosophy? What distinguishes philosophy from other fields of knowledge? What is the relation of philosophy to theology? What precisely is meant by Christian philosophy? What has it meant in the past? What does it mean here and now? What can and should be said of its future? Many of Father Smith's thoughts on these questions are expressed in the papers contained in this volume.

In the first paper, "What Is Philosophy About?" Father Smith is explaining to teachers from many departments, just what philosophy is in relation to other fields of knowledge. He starts by observing that though we all love to know, there is sometimes a block to our knowledge: we do not always know who is talking and whether the talker is right. That is, we don't always know the answer to the query, what are the facts?

Distinguishing these two possible meanings of that query: "What are the facts of the matter?" and "What are facts?" Father Smith says that philosophy will not teach us what the facts are, but it will help to remove a block to our knowledge by showing that facts are of different kinds and that different kinds of facts are relevant to different fields of knowledge.

We must distinguish between a thing and the aspects from which the thing can be viewed. We must also distinguish a kind of knowledge from the *use* of a kind of knowledge. Father Smith discusses both the good consequences that follow from knowing these distinctions and the confusion that follows from ignoring them. He stresses that in having as one of its functions to teach us what kind of fact it is that makes each field of knowledge distinct from the others and valid within its own sector, philosophy cannot be accused of imperialism; for philosophy itself is controlled by being that it sees as a given which is-but-need-not-be-given.

From "What is philosophy?" of Section I, the discussions of Section II move on to the question: "What is Christian philosophy?"

"Mr. Adler and the Order of Learning" begins as a comparison of Mortimer Adler's views with a Catholic theory of education, but it soon becomes focussed on the critical issue of the meaning and validity of the notion of a Christian philosophy.

Two groups, Father Smith says, can consistently deny the validity of a Christian philosophy: (1) Naturalists, because they think theology vitiates philosophy by making it Christian, and (2) Calvinists who, by denying the competence of reason, think that a purely natural philosophy is impossible.

But a Catholic who neither denies nature to exalt supernature nor denies supernature to exalt nature, cannot reject the possibility of a Christian philosophy. He must maintain that reason is competent and also that grace is necessary to restore it, since fallen reason needs the aid of faith in its task of being reasonable. A Catholic would not hold merely that faith *was* needed in constituting a Christian philosophy, but also that it *is* needed now in the exercise of knowing demonstrable philosophical truth. After a careful discussion of the Christian description of Christian philosophy, the essay concludes with an analysis of a relevant text from St. Thomas.

In "The Position of Philosophy in a Catholic College" the relation of philosophy to theology is quite fully discussed. This question is raised: If soul-saving is our main task, why busy ourselves with saving our minds by studying philosophy? The answer suggested is this: so long as we commit ourselves to the good as we see it, any occupation can be soul-saving. But when exercised in charity, philosophy has a special pre-eminence over other natural wisdoms since its object, being, is open to the knowledge of God. Christian philosophers have seen that the secret of the world is the fact that it exists, and the key to that secret is the knowledge of a cause of existence, but it was through Revelation that they discerned that secret and the key to that secret. Christian philosophy thus owes its existence to Revelation and would not continue in existence without dependence on the faith which created it. But this does not mean that faith should be substituted for the work of intelligence, or that philosophy has been turned into theology. As in the previous paper, the point is made that

Revelation is not needed to specify philosophical truth; it is needed for the *exercise* of philosophical wisdom.

By explaining the relation of nature to grace, Father Smith shows that though Catholic philosophy *exists* only in Catholic theology, it exists there *as* philosophy, according to its own contours, yet fresh and new, the same but renovated.

An example of Christian philosophy, so understood, can be seen in Section III, in "Philosophy and the Unity of Man's Ultimate End." Father Smith calls our attention to those moments in which men make their decisions for or against a moral good. He gives the metaphysical basis of such moral commitments and then points to the mystery involved in the question: How do we find our total infinite good in a finite instance of the good? His comments on this question and on its relation to the unity of man's ultimate end, express the insight and the vision of a Christian philosopher.

The concluding papers, in Section IV, consider the past and the present of Christian philosophy in order to look towards its future.

"A Note on the Future of Catholic Philosophy" begins with a graphic description of modern man's feeling of being lost in space, lost in time, lost in the unconscious, and lost in evil. Though his basic and anxious question, "Who am I?" does have an answer in Catholic doctrine, that answer seems unaccepted by—perhaps unacceptable to—his modern mind. Father Smith asks why this is so.

He suggests that the answer in part is this: that since in fact Catholic philosophy was created by Catholic theologians as an answer to theological needs, it is difficult for non-Catholics—and even for Catholics—to know whether a theologian or a philosopher is talking when a theologian philosophizes. We need a Catholic philosophy, Father

Smith says, which is written not for theological but for philosophical purposes. Though not venturing to state what the identification tabs of such a philosophy would be, he says that it must exhibit a full appreciation of all relevant data, as, for example, one finds in *The Phenomenon of Man* by Father Teilhard de Chardin. Written by those who have the faith but for the purpose of understanding better, not the dogmas of faith, but creatures themselves in their relation to God, such a philosophy would present to the world a new face and a more winning face as well.

In "An Appraisal of Scholastic Philosophy" Father Smith reminds us that the starting point of the scholastics' thinking was their faith. But when their metaphysics was detached from the theology that inspired it, both it and the theology from which it was isolated, were the worse for the separation. Father Smith is critical of philosophizing about the formal objects of philosophy and theology as if they were separated from the Christian's philosophizing *esse* by which they exist.

In speaking of the present, Father Smith finds that Scholasticism is more aware of its nature now than it was in the twenties. Thanks to Gilson and de Lubac, Scholasticism has, he thinks, recovered the proper maximization of the notion of the pure act of being. It has also recovered its counterpart, the maximization of the notion of human nature that is open to return by its knowledge and love, and by grace, to the God from Whom it has issued.

As to the future, though Christian theology must have a philosophy, there is no absolute necessity that its philosophy be scholastic philosophy. Nor is Thomism necessarily the only port in the storm. Thomas never meant that his name should be used to circumscribe truth. Then, too, some modern men dislike the dialectical mode of discourse used by Thomists. Yet it is good to remember, as Father

Smith tells us through Rousselot's words, that Thomas himself was not bloodless and abstract; whatever is human he loved, understood, and enjoyed.

Those who know the books of Father Smith, for example his *Philosophy of Being* (New York: Macmillan, 1961), his *Natural Theology* (New York: Macmillan, 1951), *The Truth That Frees* (Milwaukee: Marquette University Press, 1956), have seen the philosophizing *esse* of a Christian philosopher at work. In the papers contained in this book they will see his statement of what Christian philosophy is.

Beatrice H. Zedler

Marquette University
Milwaukee, Wisconsin

*Philosophy and the
Knowledges of Man*

I. Philosophy and the Knowledges of Man

What Is Philosophy About?*

I should like to give a partial answer to this question, what is philosophy about? The difficulty of this task is like the one which often confronts surgeons: they can't operate until the infection clears up, and the infection won't clear up until they operate. Just so, I can't well tell a man what philosophy is until he knows some philosophy, and no one will know philosophy until someone tells him about it. What to do? Perhaps, like surgeons who start operating and hope for the best, perhaps I had better start by philosophizing a bit, with the hope that you'll see what philosophy is about from having seen a bit of it in operation.

* This paper was given as a lecture, under the title, "The Knowledges of Man," at Marquette University, Milwaukee, on October 29, 1958. It was one of the lectures in a series (given by some members of the Liberal Arts faculty) entitled, "Worlds Without End." On March 18, 1962, this lecture was also given for the Annual Aquinas Day program at Loyola University, New Orleans, under the title, "What Is Philosophy?"

The starting point, the first surgical cut or nick I wish to make in you, is to have you realize that we all love, simply love to know. Watch your children. They are continually pestering you with questions: "Mama, why is that man bald? Daddy, why do you put two jiggers in when Mama is not around? Where does the light go when it goes out?" And when they are not pestering you, they try to find out the answers to their questions on their own: "How would it be if I cut up Mother's new formal for a dress for the doll? I wonder if Daddy's electric shaver would shave the dog? What would happen if I stuck my finger into the lawn mower, or jumped off the roof?" The results of their investigations, personal or through consultation, are often more or less disastrous. No matter. They must find out, and they do. Or watch yourselves. In the matter of wishing to know, we are just grown up children. Of course we don't wonder any more about all the problems which bother children. We know now what fire feels like. However, we keep on wondering about things, and thank heaven we do. For, if we ceased to wonder, that would mean not only that we are no longer children, but also that we have ceased to be men and women. Indeed, even sin and sanctity are a matter of wishing to find out. Our mother Eve wished to find out what would happen if she took just one teeny weeny bite of the forbidden fruit; and if she had not taken that bite, she would have refrained because she was wondering what would happen if she did *not* take that bite. Indeed, even the errors we fall into have their source in our love of knowledge. Rather than have no answer at all, we take any answer. Rather than say nothing when we have nothing to say, we will say something even if it be wrong. Rather than not make any *pas*, we will make a *faux pas*. We simply hate to admit that we don't know. This, too, is love of knowledge, a disordered love of course, but love nonetheless; a love so ingrained in us that we will sometimes accept in the place of the real thing even the appearance of knowledge. So it remains that we all love to know.

If the conditions for learning were ideal, we would all eventually and to a greater extent than we do now, satisfy our love of knowledge. The conditions are not always ideal. Lack of time, of interest, of talent, poor teachers, no teachers at all, no opportunity, no money, and so on, all these block or obstruct the path to knowledge. But even when conditions are ideal, as they are in a school, there is still a block to knowledge of which we might be quite unaware.

I shall now explain what that block is. Let me put it in its most recognizable form first. The first shape our block takes is this: we don't always know who it is that is doing the talking. An explorer, for example, recently returned, say from the North Pole, will inevitably be invited to tell his story to some audience. He may even invite himself by writing a book. In the course of his communication he may be moved to make a few remarks about the political situation, about the poetry of Shelley, or about nuclear physics, or what not. Do we know who it is that is talking when the explorer steps out of his field? Is it the explorer still? Or the critic of Shelley? Or the nuclear physicist? Not knowing who is doing the talking, we don't quite know whether to trust him, and so we can't be quite sure whether he is right or not. This is the simplest form of the commonest block to knowledge: we don't know whether a man who is talking is everything he claims to be.

There is a subtler form of that same block, yet it is exactly the same block. If we can see that the subtler form of it is exactly the same block under a different guise, we shall be better prepared to know what philosophy is. Let me get at this subtler form in this way. Assume that we are told by our explorer that, besides being an explorer of the Arctic, he is also a critic of Shelley, a scientist, and a political philosopher. Now we feel safe in trusting him. Are we? Do we really know whether what he says in these other fields is true or not? Now, this question, namely, is our explorer right or wrong in his remarks about the fields he knows *besides* the fields of his explorations: this is in a way exactly the same question as the first one, viz., who is doing the talking? And for this reason. No man purports to be talking off the top of his head. When pressed to justify our convictions, every manjack of us will say: "The reason why I say what I'm saying is the following." Note this well: the reason anyone adduces for being right is not based upon his own sayso. That reason always purports to be the facts of the matter and the necessary conclusion from those facts. Who, then, is really doing the talking? The facts of course. And are the facts as he describes them? Only the facts can tell us, and so it is still facts which are talking even in the words which describe them. Thus, the two questions, who is talking? and, is he right? are really the same question, namely, what are the facts? Facts alone speak, no matter who is doing the talking, no matter what words are being used to describe them.

This brings us to the question, what are facts? Here we are faced with a third subtlety. There is a difference between these two questions, what are *the* facts of the matter? and, what are facts? Anyone who knows them can marshal and present *the* facts which support his conclusions. But not everyone knows what sort of thing he is adducing when he adduces the facts. If, for example, I were to tell you that this table top is 4 ft. x 2¼ ft., you would know the fact, which is the measurable table top, and the table top's measurement, which is 4 ft. x 2¼ ft. I have shown you *the* fact, the table top, and by measuring it, the table top's size. This is simple enough. Suppose now I say, this table top is quarter-sawed oak. I have again appealed to a fact, namely, the kind of wood of which the table top is made. But can this different sort of fact about the same table speak to you in terms of its size? Scarcely. Any kind of wood could have exactly the same size, and you will never know from the size of it what the table top is made of. Now if a table top's size and the kind of wood it is made of are both facts, are they the same kind of fact? Certainly not. You won't learn size from the *kind* of stuff which has size, nor will you learn the kind of stuff you're dealing with from the *size* of it. This means that facts are of different kinds.

One thing, then, among others, which philosophy teaches is this: of what kind or sort are the facts which are relevant to the various fields of knowledge. Philosophy will not teach us what the facts are. Experience, observation, common sense, simply living under the same sky, all these will teach us what the facts are. Philosophy won't. Not that philosophy is not intensely concerned with the facts. Indeed there wouldn't be any philosophy unless it knew the facts, but it is not philosophy which teaches us facts. Rather, philosophy teaches us, first of all, what kind of fact subtends each field of knowledge. For instance, a sociologist will tell us that war divides men, and peace unites them. So it does. This is a fact. A philosopher will tell you what unity is, and what kind of unity and what kind of division comes from war and peace. An economist will discourse upon the nature of money. A philosopher will discourse upon the social nature of man, who needs money if he is to flourish today. A biologist will discourse upon living beings, classifying them, dividing and comparing them. A philosopher will try to tell you what sort of thing a living thing is. Put it this way: the various sciences are pyramids of knowledge. Now take one such pyramid and examine its base. That base is resting upon a fact or facts. One of philosophy's tasks is to tell you what sort of fact the pyramid is resting upon, what is the territory upon which it stands. Philosophy won't teach you chemistry, or mathematics, or economics, or any of the sciences. Philosophy will teach you what kind of fact it is which makes each field of knowledge distinct from every other, and valid within its own sector.

At this point my task of telling you what philosophy is about is somewhat done, but as an old teacher I have few illusions. I know you have not quite seized what I have been saying, and for this reason: I have not quite succeeded in saying it.

What is philosophy? It is not mathematics, or physics, or biology, or chemistry, or history or anything else but itself. It is a first step, which is this: *checking* the facts which subtend all knowledges. That first step is not the facts. It is rather to know what sort of fact you are dealing with, what sort of fact you are checking. Just as you must know a man's name before you can find his telephone number, so here, you must first know the name or kind of fact in question, before you can find it. *Then* you can find it. If you don't know what you're looking for, how can you know you've found it? Just so, if you don't know what sort of fact is relevant to, say, biology, how can you know whether there is a biology? Certainly, a mathematician treats all things as if the fact that some things are alive is irrelevant to mathematics. And so it is. The fact that your children are smallish cylindroids, have a certain height, weigh whatever they do weigh, is largely irrelevant to a biologist; but not to a mathematician; and the fact that your children are featherless bipeds or mammalian primates is irrelevant to a mathematician but not to a biologist. The facts in each field are not at all irrelevant to that field. Indeed, they are the very stuff out of which a field of knowledge is made. But that stuff itself, the facts I mean, is of various *kinds,* and it is the kind of facts in each field which it is necessary to know if we are to have a unified intellectual life. Philosophy attempts to teach us the kind of facts relevant to each field.

Let me now say the same thing in another way. Centuries ago someone stuck his head out of the window, or so the story sounds, and said, "Everything is fire;" another, same props, said, "Everything is earth;" still another, "Everything is water;" and a last, "Everything is air." It seems that these strange men then withdrew their heads and were never heard of thereafter. What on earth did they mean by such seeming nonsense? They meant that everything, absolutely everything, has something in common with everything else; for if it didn't you couldn't know thing two after having known thing number one, because if thing number two has by hypothesis nothing in common with thing number one, you couldn't know thing number two. Indeed, you couldn't even have known thing number one, because thing number one had nothing in common with anything else either. Against the fact, because you do know thing number two and one. Were these old sages right then? Dead right. They were wrong only because they pitched on the wrong thing that everything has in common with everything else. Not everything is fire, or earth, or air, or water. But everything that exists exists, and this is what everything has in common with everything else: it is a being. A fifth man, Parmenides of Elea, said that, and we have been living upon the intellectual capital of that saying of his ever since. No man,

Plato reminds us, dares lay a parricidal hand upon Parmenides, the father of all those who think. Here again we have a clear-cut indication of the difference between *the* fact and a fact or what sort of thing a fact is. *The* facts are that only fire is fire, only water is water, and so on. Furthermore, *the* fact is that everything is a being. But the *kind* of fact according to which not everything is fire, but only fire is fire, is not the same kind of fact according to which everything is a being. That every being is, is indeed a fact, but it is a different kind of fact from the fact of fire, of earth, etc.; it is a fact without which you couldn't think at all; for if not everything is a being, you wouldn't be sure that fire is a being. Thus, everything is a being, though not a fire-being, and so the pre-Socratic who said that everything was fire was wrong, and he who said that everything was water was also wrong. But they were, all of them, dead right in thinking that everything has *something* in common with everything else, and that "something," as Parmenides saw so well, is this: everything is an existent. Now, the kind of fact relevant to the truth that everything is a being is not quite the same kind of fact as that which is relevant to the truth that fire is fire.

At this point you will be saying, "All right, all *right*, what kind of fact is it that everything is a being in some way or other, and how does it differ from the fact that fire is fire, earth is earth, and water, water?" The answer needs a full dress course in metaphysics if it is to make sense. Meanwhile I may say this much in answer to the query. The kind of fact we are speaking of when we say that every thing is a being is a kind of fact *which is given but need not be given.* No other fact is of that kind. That fire is fire is given and must be given. That there *is* fire is given, but it need not be given. Now, from the given which need not be given arises the question, why is the given given at all, and the answer to that question is philosophy of one kind or another.

If all this seems difficult to follow, the reason is because it *is* difficult to follow. It is not my purpose here to teach philosophy or to clear up difficulties. My purpose is simply to state what philosophy is about. To repeat, one thing philosophy is about is the job of pointing out that relevant facts are of different kinds; that different kinds of facts are relevant to different fields of knowledge; that if we do not know the particular kind of facts relevant to a particular kind of knowledge, the process of learning is bound to end up in fruitless discussion and in a bitter scepticism, except for those who are able to take refuge with logical positivism in saying there are no problems at all outside of logic, or with semanticism in saying that all problems are a matter of words.

If, however, we do know what kind of fact is relevant to a field of knowledge, we have taken the first step in checking the facts. Suppose, for instance, some one steps out of a hearse and says, "The physical world is finite." (I am still trying to explain what philosophy is about.) "Finite" means anything that stops somewhere; "physical world" means the kind of stuff you kick around, or which kicks you around. Now watch. First of all, as I have said, the one who announces the proposition that the physical world is finite is speaking not in his own name, but in the name of the physical world. The physical world is talking through the voice of the one who is speaking. It is the physical world which is saying through the speaker's voice, "I am finite." We now ask the physical world, "Why do you say this?" One of its answers might be this: "Because I have been measured, and I have run out of anything more to measure." Clearly, the kind of fact in question here is a fact which purports to have been verified in experience, the experience of actually measuring the physical world and of finding out that there is nothing more to measure. If this is the reason why the physical world is finite, it is obviously no reason at all, because nobody to date has ever measured the size of the physical world; and the point is that the kind of fact in question (actual measurement) is not true, precisely because no one ever actually measured the physical world. The kind of fact relevant to the finiteness of the physical world, namely its actual measurement, is not there.

Let us now view the matter in another way. Suppose the physical world now answers our question, "Why do you say you are finite?" in this way: "I am finite because, even though no one ever measured me, nevertheless if anyone did measure me, he would find the following data. My actual size is finite—for any one actual size or number must be finite, yet I could be bigger than I am, because any big thing can be a bigger thing. But no matter how much bigger I can be, I cannot be so big that I exhaust the very possibility of being bigger than I am, and *since* I can't exhaust that possibility, I must somewhere actually run out of stuff of which I'm made and which can be measured." In short, the physical world may say, "You may keep on adding to my size, but since you can't add so much to me that there's nothing more to add, it follows that the stuff *to* which you have added, namely 'me,' must always stay finite in size." What kind of fact is talking now? Not the kind of fact which is verifiable in experience. Rather, the fact than an *actually* infinite size or number is an impossibility, a contradiction in terms; this is the kind of fact which is talking now. A mathematical fact is talking, or, if you will, a philosophical fact concerning the nature of size. It cannot be verified in our experience, but it doesn't need to be, for we know without such verification that a given size must be finite, because if the size were not finite, then there isn't any size given at all.

Now view another statement of the physical world. Suppose the world said, "I am infinite." (This old world can say some strange things.) Here the world cannot, as we have just seen, mean that it is *actually* bigger than any conceivable size, for then a conceivable size would be the biggest possible, and that is impossible, because a conceivable size can always be conceived as bigger. However, the world could mean this: "I am infinite, because you can always keep adding to my size, and that is what I mean by infinite." The world is right. It *is* infinite in that sense, and now we have another sort of fact which you can check for yourselves, because you know what you're trying to check. Simply ask: "Is any given number or dimension such that it cannot be larger?" The answer is, "No," and if it's that sort of fact which the world means when it says, "I'm infinite," the world is dead right. Again, suppose the world answers: "I am finite, because I am created." Here the one who is doing the talking is either God, who is talking about the world and is saying this about it—presumably with truth, since He ought to know whether or not He created anything—or it is a philosopher who is seeing in the physical world no reason at all why it should exist unless it has been made. This means of course that it is still the physical world itself which is speaking through the mouth of the philosopher. And so once more, whether it be the word of God, or the word which is the world that is speaking, clearly these two words or two kinds of facts both differ in kind from each other as well as from the kind of fact which interests the physical sciences. See then this: the kind of fact adduced is essential to our knowing whether or not any proposition about the physical world is true. The facts you can check at your leisure, but you cannot check the kind of fact unless first you know what kind of fact it is which you are going to check: a verified fact? a mathematical fact? a theological fact? a philosophical fact?

Let me now indicate the damage done to knowledge when we do not advert to the kind of fact we're dealing with, when we do not, i.e., know some philosophy. Suppose you start checking the facts before you know what kind of fact you're checking. Obviously you will check nothing. You are headed for fruitless discussion, when you don't wind up in sceptical despair.

Let me make this clearer. Suppose these three facts: you exist, you have knowledge, you make things. Are these three the same sort of facts? Is to exist the same as to know? Is to know the same as to make? Is to exist the same as to make? If these three, existence, making, and knowing are the same sort of facts, then every knowledge becomes blurred, and as William James says, we shall think of the world as "one big blooming, buzzing confusion," or as Aristotle said, as a "rout in battle" where no man makes a stand. Let's get more specific. If to exist (a fact) is the same as to know (also a fact), then a man, in order to know, has nothing to do but keep on existing. If we think this is a silly sort of business, recall that one of the greatest thinkers of the world said in effect exactly that. His name was Hegel. Again, if to know is to exist, then Karl Marx is right, because he thought that there were no alternatives in the progress of man, just as there certainly is no alternative to existing except not-existing. We all keep right on existing no matter what happens to us. Alternatives, however, can only be known, and if there *are* no alternatives to action, then either there is no knowledge, or else knowledge is continued existence along the line of one existential pressure. Marx thought the pressure was economic. Again, if to know is to make, there is no science except a making science; and so all knowledge is artistic knowledge, and so we must scrap all scientific knowledge, which makes nothing. Again, if to know is to act, then there is no science of logic or ethics, which apprise us, not how we do think and act, but how we should think and act. In sum, if everything is "one big blooming buzzing confusion," the physicist should teach biology, the biologist should teach physics; philosophy is an ideology, logic is mathematics and *vice versa*; college curricula represent only personal or institutional interests, and there should be no departments of knowledge at all, or for that matter any departments of anything.

Now, it is precisely in the measure that the three kinds of facts mentioned have not been distinguished that we now have a pretty mess in most college curricula. You have all been to school. You know that when a biologist says there is no such thing as a soul, and the philosopher, together with the whole tradition of Christian thinking, says there is, you know that you came out of your classrooms pretty much like an addled egg. What went wrong here? This: the biologist had not learned on what kind of fact he was basing his conclusion, and so he never told you, and so neither he nor you know what to check. He most likely is thinking of the soul as a bit of something which he can dangle on the end of his scalpel, or perhaps as a white dampish cloud which invests the body. Not finding that kind of "soul," he says there is none, and he's right: there isn't. Or a physicist will say, "We must be careful about our application of nuclear energy, and I'm the one to tell you when to use it and when not." He is not the one. Nothing in nuclear physics can settle when to use atomic energy and when not. Only the science of conduct can tell us that, and the reason is this: the kind of fact which supports nuclear physics is not the kind of fact which supports the science of conduct. $E = mc^2$ no doubt. This is precisely the formula involved in knowing what must happen if the conditions are right, namely, an enormous bang. But the kind of fact which interests the moralist is this: things often happen which shouldn't happen at all, and that is a different sort of fact from the atomic scientist's fact. The nuclear physicist can't tell you when you should cause an explosion and when not. He can tell you how to do the job though.

I think by now that I have done enough to show you what, fundamentally, the block to our knowledge is, and how it can be removed. The block is there when we don't know the kinds of facts which make various fields of knowledge valid. Not knowing of what kind a fact is, we don't know where to begin in checking it; we don't know, that is, what kinds of facts we are going to check. If you wish to know whether a surface is smooth, the kind of fact which is relevant to finding out is not the kind of fact which is relevant to finding out what size the surface is. Just so, if you think that all facts are of the same kind, you will be trying to measure things which you should be hearing. For example, if you wish to know what A-flat sounds like, you'd better hear the note. That a note has a vibration of, say 440 (A natural), won't tell you what the note sounds like. Again, without knowing what sort of fact you're looking for, you'll be trying to see with your eyes things which you can only understand. For example, you'll be trying to see a perfect circle, and you can't, for no circle is perfect except in the mind. But you can understand a perfect circle, even though you can't see the difference between one slightly squashed and one unsquashed, even though, indeed, there exists no thing circular which isn't a bit squashed one way or another. Again, without knowing the kind of fact you're looking for, you'll be trying to check whether God exists, and since you don't see Him or understand Him, you'll say He doesn't exist. For, if God exists, you certainly can't see Him or understand Him, except to the effect that He exists. But if you know what sort of fact supports the proposition *God exists,* you'll be satisfied that *that* sort of fact exists and is enough to assure you that God exists.

Now let me make further suggestions about how the block, our inadvertence to the kind of facts we are dealing with, I mean, may be removed.

A school sets up categories of knowledge. There is the history department, the literature department, the science department, etc. What makes these departments be different departments? The subject matter of course. *That* is why there are different departments in a school.

Let us look now at the "subject matter" of a department. It is a most curious affair. I have in my hand a piece of gold. The chemistry department will say of the gold that it is *Au,* a symbol for a vast amount of knowledge about gold, its atomic weight, boiling point, and so on. The sociologist will say of it that it is a cause of union and division of groups of human beings. The economist will say that gold is a standard of value; the geologist, that it is found in certain formations of the earth. The mathematician will be interested in what its size, shape, and weight are. The man of letters apostrophizes it with "To what lengths will you not drive the hearts of men, accursed lust for gold." *(quid non mortalia pectora cogis, auri sacra fames.)* The theologian may also have his say: it is a root of evil. And so on. Each department will have its swipe at gold. Are they still talking about the same thing? Certainly. Are they all saying the same thing about gold? Certainly not.

What then *is* the subject matter of a department? Surely all departments don't have the *same* subject matter. There must be "something else," besides the lump in my hand, which is the subject matter of each department. What is that "something else?" That "something else" is the *aspect* from which each department is viewing the gold, and it is this, the aspect from which things are viewed, that causes different departments of knowledge. When a philosopher says that gold is a substantial unit, made up of parts which are *not* units, he is using a philosophical category. When a chemist says gold is *Au*, he is symbolizing the way gold conducts itself, and so he is using another category. When an artist suggests that milady should adorn her ears with gold, he is using still another category. When an economist speaks of gold as a standard of value, he is using his own category.

If you identify the lump of gold with the *aspect* from which each department views the lump, then you may indeed say that each department is studying the same thing. But now your word "thing" is equivocal, just like the word "bark" said of a tree and of a dog. What follows? This: two kinds of knowledge about gold, say the chemist's and the economist's, then begin to compete. After all, aren't they claiming to be talking about the same thing? They are. But the economist now claims to do the same "thing" better than the chemist, or *vice versa*. Then it is a question of which one talks the loudest, gets the biggest cut of the budget, hires the most teachers, builds the biggest building. Then that department which is loudest, most vociferous and intransigent in its demands will win out. The victory is then often called progress. Thus it may happen that the school with a betatron will be considered the best school. A pretty mess! What has happened is that the aspect from which a thing is viewed is confused with the thing itself; a limited area of knowledge (the aspect of a thing) is taken to be the whole area of knowledge (the thing). Since the claim to say everything about anything can never be made by the limited area itself, for that area or aspect is quite innocent of imperialism, that claim must be made by an interested party, a party who is interested only in his own field as if his were the only field. Thus we have an imperialist. And there's more to come. The interested party can make his interest flourish only if he uses his knowledge as a weapon. So he uses it as a weapon. He kills the other departmental knowledges with his own. Why not? Isn't he doing the same thing as they, only better? Clearly we must stop the imperialist by pointing out that his is not the only field of knowledge even if it be about the same thing which interests other areas.

Another way to remove the block to our knowledge may be seen thus. Interest in the *use* of a kind of knowledge is not at all opposed to interest in a kind of knowledge, yet the confusion of its use with the kind of knowledge used can wreck a school. You might be interested, say in fishing. Now, your interest may be in catching fish (use), but not in the speculative part of the art of fishing (the kind of knowledge used in fishing). Or it could be the other way about. You could be interested in knowing all about fishing, but not particularly interested in catching fish. Many fishermen have fun without catching a thing, and many who have big hauls, small boys usually, know very little about fishing. Finally, you might be interested both in fishing and in the art of fishing.

There can be grave error, however, in supposing that the use of knowledge is the same as the kind of knowledge used. The chemistry department, for example, might use its knowledge to train students who will work in industry. There's no harm in that. Quite the contrary in fact. The harm comes when one defines chemistry as something to be used in industry. Then one's "interest" in chemistry is reduced to what use one can put chemistry to, and not in the science itself. This means that the word "interest," just as the word "thing" a while back, has now become *unrecognizably* equivocal, whereas before, when "interest" meant *either* interest in the use of knowledge *or* interest in a kind of knowledge used, the word was recognizably equivocal. There's no harm in being interested in the use *and* in the kind of knowledge used; in being interested in use but *not* in the kinds of knowledge used; in being interested in a kind of knowledge but *not* in its use; for that matter, there's no harm in being interested *neither* in the use nor in the kind of any given knowledge. The harm comes when the word "interest" is unrecognizably equivocal, as when one thinks that to know chemistry is the same as to know how to use it, because then one has lost the chemistry which one doesn't use, and thus one will gradually lose even the chemistry he is using—viz., when we lose interest, as we do, in the immediate, present uses to which we put chemistry.

Now, whether one loses a science because one has confused interest in using a science with interest in the kind of thing used, or whether one loses a science because one has confused two different aspects of the same thing, the situation is quite as if a book were removed from a library shelf: it is not so much that there is a vacancy on the shelf as that the other books have closed in upon the unoccupied space. The book is thus not only lost, another book has taken its place. The lost science is replaced by another one. Sometimes this loss is all to the good. We lost alchemy and gained chemistry. But suppose we lost chemistry and regained alchemy! Thus, people are looking today to the atomic scientists to tell them when to use the H-bomb. We have forgotten our science of conduct, forgotten that only ethics or moral theology can tell us when to use the atomic bomb. So philosophy gets lost in logical positivism. So grammar gets lost in phonetics, and the boy who is told to use the word "ominous" in a sentence is justified in writing, "If you don't stop, 'ammona sock yah.'"

There is another way of fouling up curricula or the different sorts of knowledge. We foul up curricula thus: instead of dividing departments according to the various aspects from which each department views a thing, instead of separating within the now divided departments the knowledge about how to use a science from the knowledge of what you're using, we can simply decree that the history department will now take over literature, and the theologian will take over banking. Then we shall have the historian trying to write poetry and criticize literature, and the theologian trying to create justice. Here the interest of an historian is simply willful, and so is the theologian's. The historian doesn't know any literature as an historian. It may happen indeed that he does know literature, but not because he's an historian. If he doesn't, then his willfulness in teaching history as literature is bad will. The same goes for the theologian. Again, we may "unfoul" or control these willful men if not by persuasion, then by attempted dissuasion.

Lastly, a desperate situation, not willful, not confused, but simply desperately practical, may make a school call upon departments to teach home economics or domestic science. No harm in that, unless it be supposed that home economics is a department like any other. It is not.

The cause of all these confusions is a basic confusion: the confusion of the aspect from which a thing is viewed with the thing itself. There are many, many aspects from which to view any one thing. No one of these aspects is the other, and that's why we have various fields of knowledge. Now, the word "aspect" is simply a synonym for what-sort-of-fact each field is dealing with. Each field is dealing with the facts. Each field, however, is dealing with *different sorts* of facts about the same thing. If you wish to know a field of knowledge, you must first know what sort of fact it is dealing with, what sort of fact you can expect to find at the bottom of each science. Otherwise you won't recognize it when you find it.

To conclude, one function of philosophy is to teach us what kind of fact we're dealing with, upon what territory each of the pyramids of science is resting. Nonetheless, assessor and controller of each field of knowledge, philosophy would be horrified to hear anyone charge her with imperialism. An imperialist revises everything, but he is a reviser whom nobody else revises. Not so with philosophy. Philosophy revises indeed, just as any science may; but philosophy has its own reviser, just as any science has. The reviser of philosophy is being, for philosophy is the science of being. The reviser of the other sciences is the particular kind of being each science deals with.

The science of being is constantly revised by deeper if not different insights into the mystery of this kind of fact: a fact which is given but need not be given, the fact namely that the things we see and know exist. So it is that "to be or not to be?" is still the question about things which may or may not exist, and the answer to that question is still controlled by the kind of fact which philosophy is trying to answer. Far from being imperialistic, philosophy is the humblest of sciences. For it teaches the philosopher not only that, apart from the fact that he exists, he is nothing; it also teaches him that the things he studies are also, apart from the fact that they exist, nothing. And in thus making the philosopher aware of his need of going beyond these "nothings," himself and things, to the cause of them, philosophy not only goes beyond the given to their giver; it also leaves the philosopher staring at the giver with a hope that philosophy alone cannot fulfill. It is otherwise with other fields. Above the level of any other science there is nothing more to be said about anything by that science. $2 + 2 = 4$ is the end of the line for an arithmetician when he performs that operation of addition. That there are four things is not the end of the line for a philosopher. He does not have that easeful functioning of knowledge which a mathematician has. He must go beyond the nature of numbers and sizes, beyond the categorical descriptions and qualitative properties of natures, beyond everything explicative of nature, until he comes to the explanation why nature exists. And when he has reached that explanation he would like to know more, but at that point philosophy cannot teach him more. If, then, there is humility in any scientist, because he must allow his thinking to be controlled by the kind of thing he is thinking about, that is greater reason for humility in a philosopher who is thinking about a kind of fact which is explained by a giver of that kind of fact but who Himself is not explained.

Philosophy, then, is as humble as any science, because like any science, it is not interested primarily in what men say but in what they are talking about. "*My* notion, *my* idea, *I* think," these are all prideful words about oneself, as useful as is the academic warpaint of cap and gown in assessing what a Ph.D. knows. Philosophy is even humbler than any other science, or should be, because when it comes to the point of having seen that the given-which-need-not-be-given comes from a giver who must be, it stares as a beggar with hopeful but anxious eyes fixed upon God, knowing full well that any further increment to his knowledge must be an increment he has never known and never can or will know unless God Himself gives the increase.

Philosophy and Theology

II. Philosophy and Theology

Mr. Adler and the Order of Learning*

The Order of Learning by Mortimer Adler is an excellent piece.[1] Catholics know, Mr. Adler tells them, the basic principles governing the order of things taught and the teaching of them. They know (1) the difference between intellectual habit and sensitive memory, even though they often violate that truth by putting a premium on memory instead of intellectual habit. They know (2) that intellectual habits can be formed only by intellectual acts on the part of the student, not simply on the part of the teacher. This principle they often violate by proceeding as if the teacher

---

* This paper was given at the meeting of the National Catholic Educational Association in Chicago, April 7, 1942, and printed in the N.C.E.A. *Bulletin* XXXIX (August, 1942), pp. 140-162. It was a response to a paper given by Mortimer J. Adler at a meeting of the Western Division of the American Catholic Philosophical Association, April 19, 1941. In content, because of the basic principles it expresses, it goes beyond merely an "occasional piece." The paper was reprinted in *Jesuit Educational Quarterly* VI (March, 1944), pp. 205-221.

[1] Mortimer J. Adler, *The Order of Learning*, reprinted from the *Moraga Quarterly* (Autumn, 1941), pp. 3-25.

were the only cause, and as if the learner could be entirely passive. Despite the fact that they subordinate the liberal arts to a supposed mastery of subject matter, they know (3) that the intellect, dependent as it is upon sense and imagination, can be swayed and colored by passion. They know (4) that intellectual virtues are a mean between dogmatic affirmation in excess and skeptical denials in defect. Nevertheless they try to do the impossible: give students possession of truth without perplexing them by the issues which truth resolves.

Mr. Adler then sets forth the order of learning in two theses. The first thesis is "simply that mastery of the liberal arts must precede the mastery of fundamental subject matters, which constitute the matter of the speculative virtues. Though wisdom comes first in the natural order of virtues—graded according to their intrinsic excellence—the arts, least of the intellectual virtues, come first in the temporal order, the order of human development."[2] That the mastery of liberal arts does not precede mastery of speculative subject matter in Catholic schools is evinced, according to Mr. Adler, by the fact that logic is taught in them as a science, not as an art. For, if it were taught in Catholic schools as an art, it could not be divorced, as it is, from grammar and rhetoric; nor should Catholic graduates be unable, as they are, to write and read better than their secular fellows.

Mr. Adler's second thesis concerns the ordering of means to the virtue of wisdom, the order of learning in the field of speculative virtues. (His case in point is the teaching of philosophy.) In this ordering, the subjects to be taught should follow exactly the reverse of the order of the knowability of those subjects *secundum se*. Thus, theology, metaphysics, philosophy of nature, of man, science,

[2] *Ibid.*, p. 11.

is the order of subjects better knowable *secundum se*. Reverse the list and you have the order of the better knowability of those subjects *quoad nos*. It is in this last order that subjects should be taught and learned. Why? Because teaching is Socratic, and learning, whether by instruction or discovery, is an activity of the learner. "The significance of this point . . . may not be grasped unless it is put into contrast with the now prevalent error. Today, in most cases, teaching proceeds as if the order of teaching should follow the order of knowledge, the objective order of knowledge itself, even though we know that this objective order cannot be followed in the process of discovery. In fact, it is completely reversed. Instruction which departs from the order of discovery also departs from the order of learning, for the way of discovery is the primary way of the mind to truth, and instruction imitates nature in imitating discovery. The objective structure of knowledge in no way indicates the processes of the mind in growth. Now the order of discovery is primarily inductive and dialectic, not deductive and scientific."[3] Whence, "the methods of teaching any subject matter should be primarily inductive and dialectical, rather than deductive and simply expository, for the former method is a conformity of teaching to the order of learning, as that is naturally exhibited in the order of discovery, which teaching must imitate as a co-operative art, whereas the latter method is a conformity of teaching to the order of knowledge itself, and this is an order which should not determine teaching, for it does not determine learning."[4] Whence, also, teaching must be Socratic, for only thus can it avoid the substitution of verbal memory for intellectual habit. Such teaching will outlaw, for the most part, lectures, which are largely deductive and

[3] *Ibid.*, p. 21.
[4] *Ibid.*, p. 22.

analytic; it will also outlaw textbooks, which are manuals for the memory, rather than challenges for the mind. Further, since few teachers are Socrateses, and since some books must be used, the only books which can be used to good effect are the greatest on any given subject. The test whether all this is being done is whether or not the teacher himself is learning.

All this is eminently good stuff, excellently argued and speaking straight from the shoulder. We all needed to be told it, and we cannot better the telling. Nor should I care to impugn Mr. Adler's estimate about what is going on in Catholic schools.[5] Nevertheless I disagree. Mr. Adler's order of learning seems to be seriously defective.

Before proceeding to discuss what seems to be defective in Mr. Adler's theory of education, it may be well to add that a disagreement with him over anything less than a fundamental issue would not be worth noting; still less should I presume to oppose his theory upon grounds which are my purely personal opinions. It is the Catholic philosophy of education, I think, which opposes Mr. Adler's. Lastly, if the issues between Mr. Adler's and the Catholic philosophy of education are fundamental and opposed, it would be naive to suppose that he does not know all about them. It is not he who needs to be apprised of the differences between his theory and ours; it is rather some Catholics themselves.

Catholics cannot disagree with Mr. Adler about the invariability and universality of the ends of education. Nor would any one, it may be supposed, care to maintain that Catholics always use the right means to true ends. Further, one must agree with the author of *The Order of Learning*[6]

---

[5] I should wish indeed to be sure that Mr. Adler is always speaking from first-hand information about Catholic schools. I rather think he has well-founded suspicions about how they do their job, just as I have suspicions, well founded, about how St. John's is doing its job.

[6] *Op. cit.*, pp. 11-16, 17-24.

that in the dimension of means to education, liberal arts are ordered to speculative subject matters;[7] that methods of teaching should follow the order of learning; that the order of learning is the order of discovery, which is primarily inductive and dialectic, not deductive and scientific. All this is excellently argued and speaks the plain truth. There is no disagreement in these matters.

The disagreement is rather attendant upon a paragraph which closes with the following sentence: "Philosophy can be called Catholic, then, only in the order of discovery, not in its logical structure, for as philosophy its ultimate principles are all rational and natural."[8] (Doubtless Mr. Adler would say the same of any academic subject which can be called Catholic. We may, however, as he does, confine the matter mainly to philosophy.) Let us, then, focus the point at issue. Mr. Adler maintains, and rightly, that the order of teaching must follow the order of learning, that this order of learning is primarily the order of discovery, which is inductive and dialectic, not deductive and scientific.[9] On the other hand, he maintains that "truths which pagans could not discover, can be taught to, and learned by, pagans, once

[7] Although ordered to speculative subject-matters, liberal arts are not unqualifiedly without content (vd. *op. cit.*, p. 14). Liberal arts obviously contain their own wisdom, itself ordered to speculative wisdom. Besides, speculative matters get into knowledge, by way of the liberal arts, through faith, opinion, and enunciations. Nor can one legislate to the effect that no one may learn judicatively from great books, even when those books are just bones to puppies. Sometimes, *mirabile dictu*, the puppies learn. Even though it be true, therefore, that the arts cannot be acquired except through representative subject-matter, it is also true that they cannot be acquired without some assimilation of that same subject-matter. It seems quite anti-Thomistic to empty liberal arts of all speculative content: *Sensibile in actu est sensus in actu; intelligibile in actu est intellectus in actu.* Mr. Adler, of course, means only to emphasize the difference between liberal arts and the speculative wisdom at a time when such emphasis is doubtless needed: I also wish only to emphasize the presence, somehow, of speculative content in the liberal arts, against the time when his emphasis might, unintentionally of course, reduce liberal arts to a mere practice scrimmage. The fact is, when there is question of human acts the score is always kept and it always counts.
[8] *Op. cit.*, p. 5.
[9] *Ibid.*, p. 21.

Christians have discovered them."[10] It would be unworthy of any one to understand Mr. Adler's meaning perversely. For the purpose, nevertheless, of explaining the real point at issue, I am going to allow myself a fling into perversity. Consider the situation created by saying (1) that truth must be discovered, (2) that the truth discovered can be taught to, and learned by, pagans, once Christians have discovered it. Pagans, according to a perverse understanding of Mr. Adler's meaning, pagans, who could not discover philosophical truth and who can learn it only, primarily, by discovery—just as any one else must learn—can discover philosophical truth if some one else does. Is not this (recall, I am being designedly captious) to do in principle precisely what Mr. Adler with considerable truth accuses Catholics of doing in fact? He is saying that every one must learn inductively and dialectically; that so, also, must pagans learn; that pagans could not make the inductive discovery; that they, nevertheless, can make it if some one else makes it. Do, then, pagans, who must learn by induction, learn by some one else's induction? If they do, how can they? since learning is inductive. If they do not learn by some one else's induction, but learn, nevertheless, it must be by deduction, if we are not to appeal to their human faith or opinion. Whence, in principle, pagans must resort to the very deductive principle which Mr. Adler repudiates in fact. May one fear that induction is thus turning into deduction after all?

Not if we can eliminate the awkward situation. (Here perversity ceases.) The situation in which pagans can learn by discovery, as any one must, the truths which they could not discover, or, to vary its description, the situation created by having pagans deduce truths which, in order to be learned, must be induced, can be saved by allowing that

[10] *Ibid.*, p. 5.

what one man discovers another can discover as well. That is, we might say that Man X can discover from Man Y, even though X does not discover in the same way as did Y. This would eliminate the awkward situation.

It is permissible, however, to ask if induction made from induction *in that way and about the matter in hand* will work. One may ask, in other words, whether philosophic truth, which must be primarily induced in order to be learned, can be learned by those who do not make under the proper conditions of its exercise, the very induction which teaches. Variant expressions of the difficulty are as follows. Can Catholic philosophy, which is Catholic only in the order of discovery and a-Catholic in the order of truths known, be taught in the *order of discovery* where precisely it is Catholic, as if it were *there* a-Catholic? Let us grant that the ultimate principles of philosophy are all rational and natural. The difficulty is not there. The difficulty is here: Are those same principles, not in the order of truths known, but in the order of their discovery, quite wholly rational and natural? If they are not, the awkward situation persists: a-Catholic truth can be discovered as a-Catholic there, in the order of learning, where it is Catholic. This, it seems, is incomprehensible if a-Catholic truth is not learned in a wholly rational and natural way. For, if the way of learning a-Catholic truth is not wholly rational and natural, then pagans cannot learn it except in the way which is *not* wholly rational and natural; i.e., they must cease to be pagans. For that matter, neither can Catholics learn such truth in a wholly rational and natural way; but the reason why they cannot so learn is because they are Catholics.

Thus we come to the very core of the difference and opposition between Mr. Adler's and a Catholic philosophy of education. The question is precisely this: Are a-Catholic, philosophical truths learned in a wholly rational and natural way? One can well understand Mr. Adler saying *yes* to the question. And his *yes* would void my late dialectical perversity and leave flawless his own logic. The truth is, there is an element involved here which neither his philosophy nor mine (may I say, our philosophy?) can prove or disprove. That element is Catholic theology, and Catholic theology must contest Mr. Adler's supposed *yes* in answer to the question, is a-Catholic truth learned in a wholly rational and natural way? Here is the dividing line between his and a Catholic philosophy of education—a line, no doubt, which he knows all about, though he does not let it appear.

What is that dividing line? Before we jump over it, let us take a short run. One cannot admire too much the skillful diagnosis Mr. Adler and Mr. Hutchins have made of our educational ills: we need philosophy. This they have maintained; in this they speak plain truth. If we concur with them, we are immediately faced with another question: whose and what philosophy?[11] There seem to be almost as many philosophies as there are philosophers. It might first be observed that, though this is true, nevertheless the multiplication of philosophies no more vitiates the validity of a philosophy than does the prevalence of moral evil invalidate the moral good. However, as often with the good, so with the true, we are *still* faced by the question, What is true philosophy?

---

[11] Mr. H. D. Gideonse (*The Higher Learning in a Democracy*, New York: Farrar and Rhinehart, 1937) is quite right in asking Mr. Hutchins this question. Until it be answered, there does not appear to be any successful issue to their controversy. I have not the illusion that the answer I, under the inspiration of E. Gilson's *Christianisme et Philosophie* (Paris: Vrin, 1936), shall propose will be accepted by non-Catholics. It must be noted that Mr. Gideonse's question put to Mr. Hutchins is not meant by *him* to demand a serious answer. He seems to imply that to ask the question, what or whose metaphysics, is to answer it; for in his mind there is no metaphysics. Nevertheless, the question is serious if there be a peremptory metaphysic.

This is more than difficult to define, but perhaps the question can be asked in this way: What is an example of a true philosopher? Many could be named, among them Plato and Aristotle, but we might suggest the example of Saint Thomas Aquinas. However, two sorts of people may with reason deny the validity of adducing an example of one who was both philosopher and Christian theologian.

First, those who deny that there is a theology may also reasonably deny that theology has any place whatsoever in the constitution of philosophy. Since, moreover, theology presided over the formation of Saint Thomas' philosophy, his, so will the deniers of theology maintain, or any such philosophy is not a true philosophy. In short, men who deny the existence of God may consistently deny a legitimate place in education to a philosophy which draws its inspiration from theology. Further, if a philosophy, inspired by theology, orders and regulates the fields of human knowledge, a naturalist may well add, as he does, that, in general, the supernatural has no place in an educational program.

On the other hand, Luther and Calvin, who deny the competence of reason, may consistently maintain that a Christian has no need of philosophy. *They* may consistently maintain this, I say, because, for them, it is an impertinent task to attempt the education of a fallen reason. Better leave fallen reason alone and bend all our efforts to theology. Thus, a philosophy which purports to stand by reason alone cannot, according to the Reformers, be a true philosophy, and the philosophy of Saint Thomas Aquinas and of many others, they would say, professes to stand by reason alone. Fallen reason is incompetent to create the science which orders and makes intelligible the fields of knowledge. Thus a purely Protestant educational program should by right have place only for the study of theology.

So it is that naturalists and atheists or the strict followers of Luther and Calvin are the only ones who can consistently deny the validity of a Christian philosophy which draws to a point the fields of education. Naturalists can do this because theology, they think, not only vitiates philosophy, but, also, by making it Christian, vitiates education as well. Calvinists can do this because a philosophy that is purely natural is, they must think, impossible, and so is an education which is not purely theological. Atheists may deny supernature and exalt nature; strict Protestants may deny nature and exalt supernature. The former may deny theology; the latter, philosophy. But they are the only ones who can do these things.

A Catholic cannot. A Catholic, who believes *both* in the competence of reason and in reason's restoration by grace, cannot deny *either* the possibility of a true philosophy and with it the need of profane education, *or* the necessity of revelation in the constitution of such a philosophy and with it the necessity of Christianity in education. A Catholic cannot through despair of reason flee to God, nor can he despair of God and flee to reason alone. He may not be content, as was the Renaissance, with things as they are; nor may he be discontented with the grace which can make things as they should be. A Catholic school must have both at once, Christianity and philosophy; that is to say, a Christian philosophy. A Catholic school must have a Christian philosophy if a Catholic must hold, as he does, both that human reason is competent in its own sphere—Calvin denies this; and yet, because fallen, human reason must be restored by grace—atheists deny this. Erasmus has adequately described the proper function of a Catholic education: the establishing of a nature created good, *instauratio bene conditae naturae*. Catholic philosophy will stand or fall because it is or is not real philosophy. Catholic philosophy will be real philosophy if grace has restored the reason by which it stands; else it will not be Christian, and thus likely fail to be philosophy.

As is clear, there are two positions which a Catholic theory of education must maintain simultaneously: it must maintain that reason is competent *and* that grace is necessary to restore it. To hold this is not to say, with Calvin, that grace suppresses nature. Rather, it is to hold that grace re-establishes nature and that, thus re-established, reason really operates. It does not at all follow if reason needs grace, that with grace reason is not reason. Indeed, if nature with grace were not *still* nature, there would be no morality nor merit.[12] Just so, in the intellectual order, philosophy with revelation is *still* philosophy; Christian education is *still* education. Without revelation philosophy runs the risk of not being philosophy at all, and the education which philosophy orders runs a similar risk. Either Christian philosophy must be Christian or it is doubtful if it will be philosophy at all. Either philosophy must be philosophy or it will scarcely be Christian at all. We cannot debase reason, which was created good, nor exalt reason to the extent of refusing the remedy offered by God to heal reason's errors.[13] Whether our task be to will the good

---

[12] *Summa Theologiae*, I-II, 114, 1, ad 1: Man merits inasmuch as it is by *his own will* that he does what he should.

[13] Vd. *Sum. Theol.*, I-II, 85, 3, resp. Vd. *Conc. Vatican*, Sess. III, cap. 4, de Fide et Ratione, in *Enchiridion Symbolorum*, Denzinger-Bannwart-Umberg, Herder, 1928, n. 1789: "And faith and reason can not only never conflict with each other; each also aids and is aided by the other. The reason is: right reason demonstrates the foundations of faith, and, illumined by its light, cultivates the knowledge of divine things; whereas faith frees reason from its errors, safeguards and instructs it with many a notion. Whence, far from being an obstacle to humane arts and studies, the Church in many ways helps and furthers their cultivation. For She is neither unaware of nor despises the benefits to the life of man flowing therefrom; indeed She admits that, as they had their origin in God, the Lord of all knowledge, so, if they be rightly handled, do they, with the help of his grace, lead back to God. Nor, of course, does She forbid that such studies, each in its own sphere, use their own principles and their own method; acknowledging rather this just liberty, She makes it her especial care that they oppose not sacred doctrine and thus be burdened with error or that they transgress not their proper

or to know the truth, we know that we cannot in either case so attain the total good connatural to man that we be in no wise deficient.[14] We cannot do this without God's help. Yet with His help, it is *we* who observe the law and *we* who know. We must, in short, acknowledge the healing which faith brings to knowledge. "This then I say and testify in the Lord: that henceforward you walk not as also the Gentiles walk in the vanity of their mind, having their understanding darkened, being alienated from the life of God through the ignorance that is in them, because of the blindness of their hearts."[15]

Only two objections can be raised to the educational purposes of restoring by faith and reason, a human nature created good. Both of these objections will arise from a confusion of knowledge considered abstractly with knowledge as it exists in the human intellect. Before stating those objections, it is well, therefore, to eliminate that confusion.

There are two problems of order we must consider. The one is concerned with the virtuous ordering of reason by acquired and infused habits. The other is concerned with the speculative ordering of knowledge in terms of principles and conclusions arranged in a hierarchical subordination. The first is the ordering of the knower; the second is an ordering of the objects known. Both objections confuse the two orders: objection one confuses the *knowing* of the knower with the objects known; objection two confuses the *objects* known with the knower's knowledge of them. The answer to both objections proceeds upon a distinction which must be drawn between knowing and the objects known, and consequently upon a distinction be-

---

ends and thus seize upon and perturb the field of faith." I have taken some liberty with the last sentence.
    Throughout this section of the text, the reader will recognize more than the inspiration of E. Gilson's *Christianisme et Philosophie*.
[14] *Sum. Theol.* I-II, 109, 2, resp.
[15] Eph. IV, 17-18.

tween the relation of knowledges in the knower and the relation of hierarchically ordered objects of his knowledge.[16]

The first objection is the following: It is impossible for secular studies, through philosophy, itself illumined, to be illumined by faith. We have and can have, e.g., no Christian chemistry or Christian mathematics. The objection misses the point. It is not a question of baptizing a philosophy, of making a philosopher see his subject by faith. That is impossible. It is a question of creating a Christian outlook upon, of having a theological viewpoint of, philosophy. Teachers and taught must learn. The question is, how? Turned from God by original and, likely also, actual sin, no man can return to God without God. Now, if in their return, teachers and taught be offered, not only the grace which exceeds, but, also, the grace which restores nature, why should they refuse the help which heals their minds and makes them to see their work for what it is, a block in the temple of truth? With the grace that exceeds nature one may save one's soul; with the grace that heals nature, teacher and taught may make their subjects a real means to salvation *and* education by rescuing them from that isolation from the hierarchy of knowledge which condemns those subjects to partial unintelligibility. Thus rescued, any subject is not only as sanctified as is the teaching of it; it is far more intelligible. Surely we cannot allow that work is sanctified by a good intention *à la* Kant (and before Kant, Abelard), as if intentions alone were good and not also what is intended. Nor can we allow that doctrinal content is quite complete without its completion by philosophy and theology. If mathematics, say, be a good and proper field of knowledge, if further, the teaching of it can

---

[16] Mr. Adler himself makes these distinctions; but he apparently does not admit the full force of their application.

be a holy task, if lastly, neither mathematics nor the teaching of it can be sanctified and properly educative without the aid of grace and reason ordering both the subject and teacher to the ultimate end of all knowledge, it becomes impossible that a fully acceptable scientific outlook be *not* a Christian outlook. The whole objection against the illumination, by faith, of reason in teaching or learning philosophy and other profane branches misses the point. No one asks that faith be substituted for science or literature. All that is asked is that teacher and learner and their subjects be properly organized, in the light of faith and reason, to ultimate ends. To think that they cannot be is to think as does a semi-rationalist; viz., we do not need grace to restore reason to its proper functioning upon properly ordered fields of knowledge.

The whole point in the last paragraph will be missed if it be thought that grace, affecting the reason which effects philosophy, which orders knowledge, must have the *immediate* purpose of eternal salvation. It is not a question immediately of saving a teacher's or student's soul. It is a question immediately of saving their education. The point is: the supernatural, affecting the metaphysics which effects order, is necessary properly to order man's intellectual life here on earth, for this is what it means to be an educated man here and now; namely, to have a properly ordered intellectual life. Now, a properly ordered intellectual life is had when grace restores the reason which then proceeds to function *as* reason and as reason *should* function. To educate in order to save souls is indeed the ultimate purpose of a Catholic school; immediately, however, a Catholic school's business is to perfect man, under faith, in terms of his human nature upon this earth. In *statu viae* that sort of maturization of man is precisely what it means to be a man. It is he, the man, perfected by acquired and infused virtues, of whom education is to be predicated. A Catholic school does not carry the immediate burden of saving souls. It could not even if it tried. It has the immediate burden of instructing in relation to the intellectual virtues and in relation also to the moral virtues in so far as the directive principles of these last are in the intellect. In short, a Catholic school teaches the virtues of being a man. To be a man is to be one of a race descended from, and fallen with, Adam, redeemed by grace, and destined to the Beatific Vision; to be an educated man is to be awake and at home in this family which is always menaced here by sin, but always saved in hope. *This* is the function of Catholic education, to make a man intellectually alive to fallen and redeemed nature.

If, now, we do need grace to restore reason, will not this make our curricula theological? This is the second objection. It must be denied. It must be denied that Christian learning is not true learning. Grace does not suppress, it restores nature. To think the opposite is to think in the purest vein of Calvinism. Good theology has nothing to fear from natural truth. In fact, good theology exhorts us to the pursuit of natural truth. And even if this pursuit can have no ultimately successful issue without revelation, nevertheless, educators even with the faith are not dispensed from pursuing truth. With faith alone one simply does not know, without work, the answers to many pressing questions. Nor does study with faith make those answers, when they are found, any less objective, any less scientific or peremptory. Who will deny that there is geometry in a façade of a cathedral? Who will deny the validity of economic theories based upon justice? Were Pasteur, Pascal, Wassermann less scientific for being Christian? The assertion that Christian learning is not real learning is *semi-fideistic*. Sigrid Undset *is* a great writer. Saint Thomas Aquinas *is* a great philosopher, Saint Teresa *is* a great business woman. They are great because Christian.

"We must, unless we think ourselves better informed about the functions of a Christian man than was Saint Augustine, have a deep love of the intellect, *intellectum valde ama*."[17] This means hard, painstaking investigation of our field of knowledge, an investigation which cannot stop short of the supreme effort to understand the reasons why there is anything to investigate. Possessed of these reasons, we can order our branch and ourselves in relation to the whole intellectual and social order of things. Thus ordered, our knowledge is unified and as intelligible as may be. Mr. Hutchins and Mr. Adler are right. They do not, however, go far enough for a Catholic theory of education. Philosophy can unify jumbled curricula, and restrain the pullulation of courses without content. But philosophy is not constituted without supernatural aid. The fallen reason of man needs the aid of faith in its task of being reasonable.

In this union of faith with reason we have the paradox of Christian education: education must be Christian, if it is to be education; education must be education, if it is to be Christian. Precisely because it is paradoxical, contradictory charges are made against such a notion of education. Is Christian education the training of a rational animal to be reasonable? Then why, it is asked, subject reason to faith? Is Christian education to develop the faith of a citizen *civitatis Dei*? Then why bother about the curricula of the *civitas mundi*? You Catholics cannot have it both ways: call your education Christian, if you must, but do not call it education; or, call it education, but do not call it Christian. It cannot be, so runs the charge, that reason aided by faith is still reason; nor can reason without faith

---

[17] Vd. E. Gilson, *Christianisme et Philosophie*, p. 145, sqq.

fail to be reason. Now, contradictory charges cannot both be true, and if both charges are false, they cannot be contradictory. There is a possibility of some union of extremes. Such a union is a fact, as I shall indicate. Meanwhile, both these denials are false. Reason with faith is *still* reason. Reason without faith *fails,* in fact and at the level of cardinal truths, to be reasonable. The truth is, a rational animal does not grow to a full rational stature without divine nurture. Pelagius thought he did. So also thought the Renaissance. Despite the confidence of the Pelagian Renaissance, fallen reason is not normal reason. Gay at the time of the Renaissance, sceptics are sad today.[18] To be alive today is no longer bliss. Three hundred years of joyous wantoning with fallen nature have but repeated, to date, the experience of the Prodigal Son. We see it all now. Having confused, once on a time, fallen with normal reason, seeing at long last the resultant confusion for what it is, viz., the result of sin, we are at the end of the Renaissance: either we return with the Prodigal or we face despair.

But a true Renaissance is still possible, if we eliminate the confusion. Reason needs the help of God. Nor may we despair, with Luther, of reason, or, with naturalism, of God. We may not despair as long as we be given the concrete example in which the extremes, God and man, meet and are resolved, the Man-God, Christ. In Him are united the two factors which make a salvific education possible: human nature and divine. For, each Christian is now a participation in the Incarnation; each Christian is a humanity divinized by grace; Christian reason is strong in the truth of God. To refuse God's strength is the suicide of reason; to refuse reason is to deny the strength of God.

---

[18] E. Gilson, *The Unity of Philosophical Experience* (New York: Scribners, 1937), p. 220, asks: "What was Hume, after all, but a sad Montaigne?"

We are now in a position to contrast Mr. Adler's and a Catholic theory of education so far forth as education involves philosophy.[19] Mr. Adler has subscribed to the notion of Christian philosophy. "The notion of Christian philosophy, to which I here subscribe, has two points in it: first, that the light of faith was, in fact, historically indispensable for the discovery of certain truths which, as such, belong to the domain of natural reason, and hence are strictly philosophical, not theological; second, that the light of faith is not similarly indispensable for the communication of these same truths, once they have been discovered; or, in other words, that whereas ancient pagans could not have discovered them, modern pagans can learn them from the teaching of Christian philosophers. If all (pagan) truth belongs to Christianity, as the spoils of the Egyptians belong to the Jews, so all (Christian) truth belongs to men in general, in so far as these truths are strictly evident or demonstrable in the light of natural reason."[20] The immediate reaction of Catholics to these weighted words might be as follows: What could be a fairer, a more accurate description of Christian philosophy than this? Indeed, Mr. Adler himself, I fancy, has been wondering all along what I can well be at in demanding that faith be as indispensable as reason is insufficient for the constitution of a Christian philosophy. Does he not himself admit this? Has he not himself said it? Not exactly. Mr. Adler says that faith *was* indispensable, etc. but *is* not similarly indispensable. Catholics must say that faith was indispensable and is similarly indispensable, etc. *now*. Mr. Adler accepts revelation as an historical fact. Catholics accept revelation not only as an historical fact, in Mr. Adler's sense, but, also, as a moral

---

[19] The points of agreement between the two theories have been indicated in our first three paragraphs, and summarized in the sixth paragraph.
[20] Mortimer J. Adler, *Solution of the Problem of Species*, reprinted from *The Thomist*, III (April, 1941), p. 364, n. 115.

necessity within the philosophical order of learning. However necessary faith may be historically, Mr. Adler contends, nevertheless, pagans can know without believing. Pagans cannot, without the qualifications to be indicated, know as believers know. This, Catholics must maintain. Both Mr. Adler and Catholics are defending the rights of reason, let there be no mistake about that; only, Catholics are defending the rights of believing reason; Mr. Adler, the rights of unbelieving reason. Doubtless, Mr. Adler is allowing the rights of believing reason, but Catholics do not allow unqualified rights of unbelieving reason. True it is that pagan truth belongs to Christianity, but Christian truth which is evident and demonstrable does not belong, so Catholics must maintain, *de jure naturae lapsae* to men in general. The despoiling of the Egyptians is a one-way, nonreversible transaction; the Egyptians cannot trade off their truth for Christian truth; they cannot in exchange for their own get Christian truth back again, not unless they become Christians. The light of faith and revelation is an indispensable and as similarly indispensable *now*, in the learning of evident and demonstrable truth, as it was *then*. The reason is: the need for faith and revelation is the same now as it was then, and it is the same for all men. That need arises from a common fallen nature. It would be strange indeed if pagans, who are by hypothesis unhealed, were to enjoy with full right the philosophical truth which Christians can enjoy because, by hypothesis, their fallen nature has been healed. Is the healing of reason, which is an indispensable condition for being reasonable, to be indispensable for Christians and not for pagans? Is pure intellectualism, which fails, to succeed where only faith-illumined intellectualism succeeds, viz., in the knowledge of the existence of God, of the immortality of the soul, and the destiny of man?

Let it be recalled once more that the need of reason, pagan or Christian, for faith, is not a point which philosophy can settle. Only theology can settle it. Nor would it be fair to appeal to the norm of theology, unless Mr. Adler had invited and, I am sure, welcomes such a criterion. The situation, then, is as follows: Mr. Adler is telling Catholics what the Catholic philosophy of education is. In his treatment and description of the Catholic philosophy of education he is right in all points but one: the Catholic philosophy of education is not what he says it is. Catholic theology asserts the need of believing what natural reason can prove. Mr. Adler denies this need of believing what natural reason can prove: "Modern pagans can learn from the teaching of Christian philosophers ... all (Christian) truth belongs to man in general, in so far as these truths are strictly evident or demonstrable in the light of natural reason."[21] This is not so: according to Catholic theology Christian truth does not belong to man in general, not even the Christian truth which is strictly evident and demonstrable. The issue is not whether Mr. Adler be right or wrong in maintaining that demonstrable and evident truth belongs to man in general. Rather, the issue is whether he be right or wrong in saying that his is the Catholic version of the matter. In other words, does his description of Christian philosophy, a philosophy which belongs to men in general without faith (i.e., pagans), fit the Christian description of Christian philosophy, a philosophy which belongs to men with faith? His description does not fit. Evidently he is not playing fast and loose with the notion of Christian philosophy. Evidently his point that Catholic schools are not always true to the ideals of the order of learning is well taken. Evidently there is a common element in his own order of learning and ours, or there should be. The serious

[21] *The Order of Learning*, p. 21.

error rather lies here: in his conception of what *Catholics* think about the role of revelation in the life of man. This is not a charge that he is wrong in maintaining that demonstrable Christian truth is open to men in general. (I believe he *is* wrong there, but that is not the point.) It is a charge that he is wrong in holding that *Catholics* think that.

They do not. Is it necessary, asks Saint Thomas, to believe those things which can be proved by natural reason? Yes, "it is necessary for man to accept by faith not only things which are above reason, but also those which can be known by reason: and this for three motives. First, in order that man may arrive more quickly at the knowledge of divine truth. Because the science to whose province it belongs to prove the existence of God, is the last of all to offer itself to human research, since it presupposes many other sciences: so that it would not be until late in life that man would arrive at the knowledge of God. The second reason is, in order that the knowledge of God may be more general. For many are unable to make progress in the study of science, either through dullness of mind, or through having a number of occupations and temporal needs, or even through laziness in learning, all of whom would be altogether deprived of the knowledge of God, unless divine things were brought to their knowledge under the guise of Faith. The third reason is for the sake of certitude. For human reason is very deficient in things concerning God. A sign of this is that philosophers in their researches, by natural investigation, into human affairs have fallen into many errors, and have disagreed among themselves. And consequently, in order that men might have knowledge of God, free of doubt and uncertainty, it was necessary for divine matters to be delivered to them by way of faith, being told to them, as it were, by God Himself Who cannot lie." Saint Thomas then answers his three objections. The first runs: it is superfluous to believe what one can know. Answer: "The researches of natural reason do not suffice mankind for the knowledge of divine matters, even of those that can be proved by reason: and so it is not superfluous if these others be believed." The second objection is that "those things must be believed, which are the object of faith. Now science and faith are not about the same object . . .". Answer: "Science and faith cannot be in the same subject and about the same object: but what is an object of science for one, can be an object of faith for another . . ." The third objection stated that "All things knowable scientifically would seem to come under one head: so that if some of them are proposed to man as objects of faith, in like manner the others should also be believed. But this is not true. Therefore, it is not necessary to believe these things which can be proved by natural reason." Answer: "Although all things that can be known by science are of one common scientific aspect, they do not all alike lead man to beatitude: hence they are not all equally proposed to our belief."[22]

Let us now review the situation. There are two orders of knowledge: the order of truths known, the order of knowing them. The order of truths known is the order of specification, the order of knowing them is the order of exercise. Saint Thomas maintains that revelation is *not* necessary in order to specify demonstrable, philosophical truth; and he also maintains that revelation *is* necessary to constitute the exercise of knowing demonstrable, philosophical truth. Is, or is not, revelation necessary to the exercise of philosophical knowledge? If Mr. Adler says, yes, revelation is necessary to the exercise of philosophical knowledge, it would seem that he must revise his version of Christian philosophy; i.e., he may not say that de-

[22] *Sum. Theol.*, II-II, 2, 4 (Dominican Translation.)

monstrable philosophical truth is open to unbelieving men in general. I mean, he may not say that *Christians* say that. If, on the other hand, Mr. Adler says, no, revelation is not necessary to the exercise of philosophical knowledge, he may not say that he subscribes to a Christian version of Christian philosophy. The rationality of philosophical truth is one thing; the rationality of philosophers is quite another. The rationality of philosophical truth is not specified by revelation; the rationality of philosophers is dependent upon revelation. If, indeed, the rationality of philosophers did not depend for its exercise, i.e., for its being rational, upon revelation, Mr. Adler's *Order of Learning* would be unquestionably true. If, however, the rationality of philosophers does depend for its exercise upon revelation, then the *Order of Learning* is not a Christian version of the same order. The Christian version is this: only believers can do what Mr. Adler asserts unbelievers can do. In short, either Mr. Adler's version of the order of learning is not Christian, or, if it is Christian, he is not subscribing to it.

To conclude, it does not seem true to say that "if we wish to avoid violating the basic Thomistic distinction between philosophy and theology, between the spheres of reason and faith, we must, in speaking of the philosophy of education, restrict ourselves to purely natural education, natural both as to ends and to means."[23] Quite the contrary: if we wish to avoid violating Saint Thomas' distinction, we must *not* restrict ourselves to purely natural ends and means in speaking of the philosophy of education. Saint Thomas asks whether it be necessary to have another doctrine beyond philosophy. He answers, yes; i.e., one must have more than philosophy, not merely in the order of salvation—rather evidently one must, if there be a super-

[23] *The Order of Learning*, p. 4.

natural order; but one must have that other doctrine coming from revelation even in the order of these truths about God which can be investigated by natural reason. In the order of these *natural* truths, he says, it was necessary that man be instructed by divine revelation. His reason is that without such revelation few men, and they very slowly and with the admixture of many errors, would come to the knowledge of such truths. Few men, slowly and with the admixture of many errors can know natural truths about God without revelation; thus is marked by Saint Thomas and after him by the Council of Vatican[24] the limit of human capacity to know metaphysics; *Ad ea etiam quae de Deo ratione humana investigari possunt, necessarium fuit hominem*[25] *instrui revelatione divina.* This Saint Thomas says in the first article of the first question of the first part of the *Summa Theologiae.*

---

[24] *Enchiridion Symbolorum*, etc. n. 1786.
[25] I.e., man in general. Mr. Adler's philosophy is not in question; extraordinary as his philosophical gifts and attainments may be—and they are truly remarkable, he cannot but be one of the few who at long last will come to philosophical truth without revelation.

The Position of Philosophy in a Catholic College*

There is a story about the three religious who landed in heaven on the same day, at the same hour, and in the same place, smack before the Holy Family. At the sight of the Holy Child the Franciscan's heart glowed, and no wonder. Son of the great St. Francis of Assisi, he saw in the Child Jesus the perfect exemplar of all the Christliness which we now name Franciscan. To Our Lady, who alone has destroyed all the heresies of the world, the Dominican turned, for the Sons of St. Dominic have, like her, preached and preserved immaculate the central dogma of Christianity, which is the causality of God: *fecit mihi magna qui potens est.* The Jesuit made straight for St. Joseph, drew

---

* This paper was given at the 29th annual meeting of The American Catholic Philosophical Association on April 12, 1955, Philadelphia, Pennsylvania. On that occasion Father Smith was presented with the Cardinal Spellman-Aquinas Medal for his achievements in the area of philosophy. The paper was therefore the 1955 "Cardinal Spellman-Aquinas Medalist's Address". It was printed in the *Proceedings of the American Catholic Philosophical Association* XXIX (1955), pp. 20-40.

him aside, and asked him: "Say, where were you thinking of sending the Boy to school?"

Jesuits have always cherished the conviction that they were running Catholic schools, or at least that they knew what a Catholic school was. I propose to examine the position of philosophy in a Catholic school, not indeed in order to call Jesuits to account—they have enough to answer for, but because, as a teacher of philosophy, I am becoming increasingly sensitive to a danger that I may soon be out of a job. Though catastrophic perhaps for me, my being fired would have little significance unless I were fired for reasons which would menace the jobs of all us teachers of philosophy. If such reasons are abroad, it seems in order that we teachers of philosophy either strike right now, or resort to some collective bargaining right now. You may take the following remarks as an effort at collective bargaining before the strike.

The menace to our jobs comes I think from two sources: from some of our colleagues in philosophy, and from some of our theologian friends. Let me describe in a simple way how this double threat arises.

If, as M. Gilson has said, a Christian education is one "given in schools in which the whole life of both teachers and pupils is informed by the love of Christ;"[1] if to love Christ is to keep His commandments ("He that loveth Me keeps My commandments"); if one may keep or break the commandments of Christ with or without philosophy, what, it may be asked, what is philosophy doing in a Christian school? Why not throw it out altogether? Doubtless our schools would turn into schools for Christian perfec-

---

[1] E. Gilson, *The Breakdown of Morals and Christian Education* (Toronto: St. Michael's College, 1952), p. 1. Cf. Pope Pius XI, *Christian Education of Youth*, New York: Paulist Press, 1930), p. 65: "The true Christian, product of Christian education . . . thinks, judges and acts . . . in accordance with right reason illumined by the supernatural light of the example and teaching of Christ . . ."

tion, but what is wrong with *that* if Christian perfection is the end of man?

Let me put the same issue in another way. At the Mass which inaugurates every academic year in a Catholic school, the preacher usually assures the students that they are in school in order to save their souls, and when the preacher leaves the pulpit everyone including himself, straightway busies himself in saving his mind, if not his soul. Why—if soul saving is their main job, and if that job can be done without saving their minds?

Two extreme solutions of our problem have often been proposed. One is to scrap philosophy, because when viewed *sub specie aeternitatis* philosophy is a waste of time. Another solution is to keep philosophy by all means, but to keep it under the baton of a theology which discreetly taps philosophy's shoulders and flanks from time to time in order to keep the beast upon its philosophical path. Clearly the first solution destroys philosophy altogether and for that matter every other study in the curriculum as well. If the second solution does not destroy philosophy, it fails to do so only upon the supposition that philosophy is given without theology, given, I mean, with all the conditions for its existence, ambling along on its own four legs (or two), and needing only an occasional joggle from theology to keep it straight. Suppose, however, that there would have been no Catholic philosophy to tap in line unless theology's baton had once been the wand which, as it once summoned philosophy into existence, now keeps it there? If this be true, a teacher of philosophy who forgot the origin and the condition for the continued existence of his subject would suffer an amnesia which would be completely disastrous. Not only would he forget the origins of his philosophy, he would no longer be able even to identify his subject: for, *non enim aliter eas [creaturas] in esse conservat, quam semper eis esse dando.*[2] Whether a creature never was in being or whether it has been annihilated, at any rate it is not around to be identified. In other words, one way of losing our jobs is to have no job to lose, and surely we have no job to lose if there be no Catholic philosophy to teach. Whether, then, we are to be fired because our jobs are useless *sub specie aeternitatis,* or because we are *now* to be made aware that we never had the job we thought, namely, one whose origin and continued existence depends upon theology, in either case we are out of a job. That it be a theologian or a philosopher who makes either suggestion is incidental to the nature of the threat: the threat comes from a deficient philosophy or a deficient theology.

There are other ways of showing theological and philosophical deficiencies in this matter. When, for example, we say that, besides busying ourselves with saving our souls, it is also good to busy ourselves with teaching and learning philosophy, aren't we really saying we have part-time jobs? Part-time jobs when we know we cannot serve two masters! And if we amend our suggestion by saying that, after all, the job of teaching and learning philosophy can be sanctified by a good intention, aren't we trying to lift the curse upon our job by decree? Strange decree which can change facts! The fact is that teaching and learning philosophy is not the same sort of occupation as soul saving. *Laborare est orare,* it is said. On the face of it the adage is not true. All of us have labored when our labor was not a prayer, and even when we have tagged our labor with a morning offering, still and all, the address on it is not the contents of the package. Just so, philosophy is not soul saving, and no one can make it so by decree.

[2] St. Thomas Aquinas, *Summa Theologiae,* I, 9, 2, resp.

The solution to our problem lies, I believe, not only in seeing that the perfection of man is the love of charity but also in seeing why it is in the name of intellectualism itself that this is so. It is in the name of intellectualism itself that this is so, for, "not only do we understand God only through Jesus Christ, but we understand ourselves only through Jesus Christ. We understand life and death only through Jesus Christ. Outside of Jesus Christ we do not understand what life is, nor death nor God, nor ourselves."[3] To understand God, life, death, ourselves—what intellectual goals surpass these? And yet this perfect and comprehensive program for an intellectual life is unattainable except through Jesus Christ. I shall now try to make clear what that means.

According to Catholic theology, nature was created *only* to serve as a substrate and organ of the supernatural life and become a living temple of the Holy Ghost.[4] In order to set this principle within the context of our topic, which is "the place of philosophy in a Christian school," replace the word "nature" with the word "philosophy." Justified, because philosophical wisdom is the very crown and perfection of the human intellect, which is the very crown and perfection of nature, this substitution now makes our principle read thus: according to Catholic theology philosophy was created only to serve as a substrate and organ for the supernatural life.

That principle may be better seen in its generality if we look at the phases or moments of the divine decision to create spirits. It is possible to think of that decision in its

---

[3] Pascal, *Pensées*, ed. L. Brunschvicg (Paris: Nelson, 1934), N. 584, p. 268. (Translation mine)

[4] M. J. Scheeben, *Handbuch der Katholischen Dogmatik*, Zweiter Band, (Freiburg im Breisgau: Herder'sche Verlagshandlung, 1878), #173, n. 990 p. 432: "Denn nach katholischer Anschauungsweise ist die Nature von Gott *nur darum* geschaffen und verliehen, damit sie als Substrat und Organ des übernatürlichen Lebens diene und ein lebendiger Tempel des hl. Geistes werde."

first phase as a decision to create spirits, and, in its second phase, as a decision to give to spirits the beatific vision of Himself. It is also possible to think that the first phase of the divine decision to create spirits is the decision of God to give Himself, and, in the second moment, as a decision to create spirits to whom He might give Himself. It is the second viewpoint, I believe, which is correct. God creates spirits, not in order to have a cheering section to which He might listen and so derive the profit of hearing them cheer; rather, He creates spirits in order that their cheering for Him might profit *them*.[5] If this is so, it is the supernatural life which dominates nature, gives nature its total meaning and goal. Hence it is to the law of grace that the laws of nature are ordered, as, for example, pharmacy is ordered to medicine. Pharmacy makes some but not much sense unless its prescriptions be devised for our health. Just so, human nature makes some but not much sense unless it be for God. And so, grace does not traverse nature as a side-road cuts into the main highway, nor does it accompany nature as two parallel highways accompany each other, neither starting nor ending as one highway. Rather, grace orders nature from the instant nature begins to be, accompanies nature as a co-principle of human acts, and crowns nature by making created spirits at last see God.

Grace does all this in two stages. First, not only by presupposing nature and all nature's existential conditions, but also, by reason of the *first* moment of God's decision to allow spirits to see Himself, by ordering according *to its own law* those conditions in nature which make nature worthy or worthier, *by* grace, *of* grace. Of itself nature is

[5] St. Thomas Aquinas, *Sum Theol.*, I, 19, 5, *resp.* ad fin.: "Vult ergo hoc [the cheering section] esse propter hoc [the end, which is Himself], sed non propter hoc [Himself] vult hoc [the cheering section]." The relation of the first *hoc* to the second is absolutely general: there is *no* cause in creatures of the divine will to create; the cause of creatures is God alone.

like a field in the sun. The field cannot by its own law either cause, or remove the obstacles to, the sun's shining. The sun shines by its own law, not the field's. Just so, a spirit, *ex suis*, cannot cause, or remove the obstacles to, grace. Nevertheless grace, according to its own law, can cause conditions in nature whose absence would be an obstacle to grace, and whose presence will make nature worthy or worthier of grace. Thus, grace supposes those conditions in nature which it itself posits according to its own law, with the result that grace is not given without those conditions, and with the result also that even if those conditions are given, grace may not be efficacious. No one by nature is worthy or worthier of grace, but by grace nature is worthy or worthier of grace.[6]

We can descry this law of grace more readily in some cases than in others. For example, it is easy to see that there are body structures which dispose one more readily to chastity, to meekness, or to some other virtue. These structures St. Thomas calls the **beginnings of virtues**.[7] Again, good health helps the supernatural life along: "you can do many works when in good health; what can you do when ill? Few are made better by sickness".[8] Again, it is better to be good before one is old, because age may hinder piety.[9] Again, although a man may try to teach from the motive of charity, nevertheless "a fool is deceived, deceives himself, and cannot teach".[10] Again, an inconstant will makes a complete supernatural life impossible.[11] All this is readily seen.

[6] C. Truhlar, S.J., "De Viribus Naturae Humanae in Vita Spirituali", *Gregorianum*, XXXV, 4 (1954), pp. 612, 613.
[7] St. Thomas Aquinas, *Sum. Theol.*, I-II, 51, 1 *resp.* ad fin.
[8] *The Imitation of Christ*, Bk. I, ch. 23.
[9] *Ibid.*
[10] L. Hertling, S.J., *Theologia Ascetica*, 2nd ed. (Rome, 1944), n. 164, p. 80. St. Thomas says: ". . . praedicare et docere sunt actus alicuius virtutis, scilicet misericordiae; unde et inter spirituales eleemosynas computantur, . . .", "*In IV Sent.*, d. 49, q. 5, a. 3, *qu.* 3, *sol.* 3, ad 1.
[11] C. Trulhar, S.J., *op. cit.*, p. 617.

It is more difficult to see nature's preparation by grace for grace in other cases. The sick, for example, are often holy, holier even, we may at times suppose, than if they were well: "I will glory in nothing," says St. Paul, "save in my infirmities;" and again, "My grace is sufficient for thee, for strength is made perfect in weakness" (2 *Cor.*, xii. 5). Jerome, it seems, had a liverish temper which made him quarrel, or try to at least, with all his friends, even with the great Augustine; and Augustine himself seems to have had no *inchoatio castitatis* in his make-up. Yet both turned out to be saints. I recall that some future martyrs of the Orient who lived with St. Aloysius found it hard to put up with him. "Today," one said in his diary, "today Aloysius did not come to the villa. *Deo gratias!*" Despite appearances, however, our natural resources, ordered by grace to grace, suit us to a T when we face the crucial disposal of ourselves in regard to good and evil and so in regard to our eternal destiny. We must not forget that although we are given talents each according to his own power *(secundum propriam virtutem)*, we are also given each his own power; and it is according to *that* power that grace will fructify.

The second stage of grace's function is to elevate the psychophysical activity of man to the supernatural order. Grace inserts itself into nature in such wise that it is man's elevated nature which is the effective principle of his salvation. When the Holy Ghost moves the mind of man to charity, this motion does not so proceed from the Holy Ghost that the mind of man is inert under the divine impact, like a body in relation to the one who shoves it; rather, when the will is moved to love by the Holy Ghost, the will itself is also the cause of this act of love.[12] Hence, if we ask, what power is performing an act of charity, we must answer, the natural power of the will as elevated by

---

[12] St. Thomas Aquinas, *Sum. Theol.*, II-II, 23, 2, *resp.*

grace to the point where the will itself is the cause of the meritorious act[13]—this is the power which causes the act of charity. A man merits by his own will.[14]

And now as to the relation of grace to philosophy. Why study and teach philosophy? What is philosophy doing in the supernatural life? Why, philosophy, first of all, has pretty much the same place in the supernatural life which any other human occupation has. For, although there are many, many reasons for not busying oneself with philosophy, quite as there are for going fishing, nevertheless, the instant one decides for or against any occupation whatsoever, a commitment of oneself to good or evil has inserted itself into one's life. This commitment of oneself to the good as one sees it, this it is which makes a man a good man. Maybe a given commitment won't make one a *very* good man. There are greatly good and slightly good men, just as there are mortal and venial sins, yet commitment to the good as one sees it makes a man good; and commitment to evil, evil. True, in committing oneself to the good as we see it, we may or may not succeed in attaining the good under the specific guise it wears; we may or may not become philosophers. Success or failure in the matter of being a philosopher depends upon causalities other than our own. Indeed the whole venture may have been a mistake from the outset. No matter. If it was a blameless mistake, the mistake was also from causalities other than our own. But commitment is from our own causality, and it is our own causality which makes us good or bad. Clearly we do not blame animals for being short or long-haired. Short, long-haired, or hairless a dog must be by a causality which

---

[13] Cf. Cardinal Billot, S.J., *De Virtutibus Infusis*, 4th ed., (Rome, 1928), p. 43.
[14] St. Thomas Aquinas, *Sum. Theol.*, I-II, 114, 1, *ad.* 1: "Dicendum quod homo inquantum propria voluntate facit illud quod debet, meretur." Cf. *Sum. Theol.*, I-II, 21, 4, *ad.* 2: "Et ideo per suum actum meretur vel demeretur apud Deum."

is nature's causality, not the animal's, and so indeed must men; but a man is a good man by his own causality, viz., by his free decision to accept the good as he sees it.[15]

What veils this mystery to our eyes is mainly and precisely the fact that the good to which we commit ourselves, and which we possess in so doing, is not fully seen by us. Rather, it is loved by us. Later it will be seen in all its splendor, but here and now it is only "the star to every wandering bark whose worth's unknown, although its height be taken". Then too, we become confused, because some commitments, such as the commitment to the life of philosophical wisdom, do not demand the surrender of sensuous goods which some of the Ten Commandments do; other commitments demand no surrender of sensuous goods at all. But it is a huge mistake to think that the difficulty of the task is always the measure of goodness of committing ourselves to it. Upon that supposition only the return of the prodigal son would be good, because it was hard. Yet we must not forget the elder son who had no difficulty about staying home minding his own business, and to whom it was said by his father, "All that is mine is thine". It might be added that, as far as difficulties are concerned, a man who meant business and knew something about the intellectual life might well prefer to be skinned alive rather than lead it. Cardinal Newman in effect said that he would.

In sum, it makes little difference, in a way, what sort of occupation a man chooses, provided only that he choose it because, all things considered, he thinks it best. "Whether you eat, or drink, or whatsoever else you do, do all to the glory of God" (1 *Cor.*, 10.31).[16] This should dispose of the

---

[15] G. Smith, S.J., "Philosophy and the Unity of Man's Ultimate End," *Proceedings of the American Catholic Philosophical Association*, XXVII (April, 1953), pp. 60-83. [This paper is included in Section III of this book.]

[16] Cf. *Rom.*, 14. 6. Cf. also St. Thomas Aquinas, *De Malo*, I, 5, *resp.*

difficulty that only the saving of his soul is the legitimate occupation of a Christian. There *is* no occupation which is not the very occupation of soul saving, because no occupation, including soul saving itself, does not involve a human act which commits a man freely to good or to evil. Positively, any and every proposal made to our power to choose is accepted or rejected by us in a free commitment which makes us good or bad men. This will move all the powers of the soul; and since the will is the subject of charity, the dominion of charity, which informs the rest of the supernatural life, is inserted into the will which moves the other powers of the soul.[17] The sons of God are free in some of their disposals of matter, e.g., they are free to choose to build a small or a big house. Grace inserts itself into that act. The sons of God are free to turn to the good. Grace inserts itself into that act. The sons of God are free to prefer eternal life to temporal. Grace inserts itself into that act. The sons of God are free in their very vision of God. Grace inserts itself into that act. Wherever liberty appears, there grace appears; and wherever grace appears, there eternity is either dawning or is at hand.

A while back it was said that it makes little difference in a way, what one does in working out his salvation, provided he does it in charity for charity is salvation. The time has now come to clarify that "in a way".

Let us stand the various sorts of men in line: the chemist, the mathematician, the philosopher, the grocer, and all the rest. Must we think that any one of these men is as

---

[17] St. Thomas Aquinas, *In III Sent.*, d. 23, q. 3, a. 1, *sol.* 1. On the relation of intellectual to moral virtues (the acquisition, cultivation and the good use of knowledge requires the will), see: *Contra Gentiles*, III, 26; *De Virt. in Comm.*, a. 7; *Sum. Theol.*, I-II, 57, 1, *resp.*: *In III Sent.*, d. 23, q. 1, a. 4, q. 1, *sed. contra*; *Sum. Theol.*, I-II, 16, 6, *resp.*; 17, 6, *resp.*; II-II, 166, 1, *resp.*; 166, 2, ad 2; 167, 2. Cf. E. Gilson, *Wisdom and Love in St. Thomas Aquinas* (Milwaukee: Marquette University Press, 1951), p. 42, n. 3; p. 45, n. 5; p. 49, n. 8; p. 54, n. 22.

well off in his occupational nature as any other? The question must be clearly understood. This is not the question: is any one any better off than another in his occupational nature *qua* elevated? Clearly, any man can be as holy as any other, no matter what they do. The question is rather this: in the order of grace, which disposes and elevates nature to the supernatural life, is a philosopher's nature *qua* philosopher's nature better than, say, a chemist's? Is the author of the *Summa* on all fours with the author of *Principia Mathematica* when both are in the order of grace, that is, when both are disposed to, or elevated by, grace? Is the philosopher *qua* philosopher better off in his nature's expectancy of grace, yes, even in his nature when elevated by grace, than, say a chemist *qua* chemist in the same situation?

Notice, first of all, that no one *loses* his occupational nature when disposed to, or when in the order of, charity. Nothing that grace assumes is lost—not if we believe in the dogma of the Resurrection. Although stamped for death, mortal things do not die forever. It is the mind which the things stamped for death touch *(mentem mortalia tangunt)*, and the mind takes everything, including the body, into eternity. All creation is awaiting the liberation of the sons of God, and their liberation is not a liberation from nature, but a liberation of nature into a state of glory, quite as the body of Christ after His Resurrection was transformed into glory. Though we shan't read the *Summa* in heaven, and still less P. G. Wodehouse, nevertheless neither of these works is completely lost in the world of grace here or hereafter. "Vanity of vanities and all is vanity," exiles from the kingdom of heaven only nature without grace, not nature with grace. With grace nothing in nature is vanity. As Bossuet said of Magdalen's love for Christ: her hair, her kisses, her perfume, every bit of her was in her love *(tout y va)* for Him. Granted all this, our question persists: is a philosopher *qua* philosopher better off when disposed to, or when in, the supernatural life than any other man?

In the sense in which all men are philosophers, no, he isn't. Every one of us has to face reality from a viewpoint which transcends or differs from the occupational angle from which we usually see it. A chemist, for example, very well knows that the elements in Mendeléyev's table, no matter how combined, will not quite describe his children, and a mathematician very well knows he cannot use his equations to settle the issue of taking or not taking a vacation. Transitive action and sensation, the *le fin fond de la nature* as Meyerson calls them,[18] these cannot be explained by the causalities of atomism, or by the formal causality of mathematics. Life is far too complicated to be understood by any one formula, nor do men try to understand life by one formula, even when they say they do. We all take things as they are, either to resign ourselves to them or to rebel against them. Should we not ever take things as they are, we would fulfill the definition of a schizo—and be locked up. Now, to take things as they are, this roughly is to be a philosopher in the sense that any man is a philosopher, and in *that* sense a philosopher is no better than a bricklayer: both eye reality quietly, competently, knowingly, with all the intellectual equipment needed by those who live under the same sky.

The professional philosopher, however—what about him? Is he better off in relation to the supernatural life than any other man? It seems so if you will allow that his philosophy is of the sort which acknowledges that the very heart of reality is the act of being which we call *esse*.

---

[18] E. Meyerson, *Identité et réalité* (Paris: Alcan, 1908), p. 366.

Let me explain. If we name reality that which exists (to date, no one has named it that which does not exist), and if we ask why reality exists, our question might be as meaningless as this one, why is a hot thing hot? For, it is self-evident that a hot thing is hot. Yet, if there be two hot things, then the question, why two, is pertinent, because you cannot explain *two* hot things upon the score that to be a hot thing is to be two of them. Just so, you cannot explain why there are two existents upon the score that to be an existent is to be two of them, because to be an existent is to be an existent; it is not forthwith to be two existents. Granted, then, that there are at least two existents, I must understand this fact as being due to a cause, and since the cause we sought was by hypothesis a cause of existents, it follows that the cause we find is an uncaused cause of existents, else it would not (having its own existence caused) be a cause of existents. What do we mean "found"? We mean, "found," as that is found which is still sought for even when it is found, as, for example, water is found by blind lions in a desert. We do not know what it is we have found when we find the cause of existence, but this much we do know: (1) we have found it; we are assured (2), that whatever it be which we have trapped in the sack of our proposition, *God exists*, it is the content within the sack which, if we knew fully, would be the optimum intelligible in whose light we could see all the rest.

It is precisely this attitude of a philosopher, the attitude, namely which he must assume when he has reached that point in his research where he can go no farther without revelation—and farther he *must* go if in knowing the cause of being he does not yet fully know what the cause of being is; it is this attitude which makes the philosopher *qua* philosopher especially open to grace, and when in grace, enhanced in his nature above all others. No other science expects anything above the level of its own viewpoint, because there is nothing *at* the level of its own viewpoint which is *above* the level of its own viewpoint. When you have learned that man is a mammalian primate, a featherless biped, or that poison ivy is *rhus toxicodendron pubescens,* or whatever, you have learned all you can in terms of what those objects feel like. Further descriptions of them in those terms will only be more of the same. So also, when you learn the size, shape, and numbers of things you can go no further than their size, shape, and number, because there is nothing more in quantity than quantity. Physical and mathematical descriptions of things are the only answers possible to the questions which physics and mathematics pose. Indeed, every science short of philosophy is closed, walled in, confined, by the very terms in which it asks its questions. Not that this is a bad situation. It simply marks the limit of their knowledges. Should a mathematician with no resources beyond his mathematics wish to transcend his field, then, as Einstein suggested with more truth than he dreamed, he might have done better by being a plumber. A plumber at least knows that his craft has not the last word to say, because he bumps into the chance event and the free event. He is not confined to the serene uneventfulness of mathematics. A philosopher, however, is not so walled in. The term in which he speaks of reality is the very term in which each and every thing speaks of itself, the term which is its being; more, the term is the very term in which God speaks of Himself: I am He Who *is*. And even though a philosopher *qua* philosopher cannot hear God speak about Himself, nevertheless, if God does speak about Himself, a philosopher is better circumstanced to understand God's language, because it is the very language which a philosopher himself has always used, the language of act, from the lowest actuation of matter by form, through the actuation of form by *esse*, up to the actuation which is not the actuation *of* anything, but act itself, unactuating and unactuated: the "Is" which is God. Moreover, besides being better circumstanced to understand God's language about God, because God's language is his own, the philosopher is also better able to speak God's language to others. For, although literature is also an instrument for communicating revelation, and in the use of this instrument the Fathers excelled, nevertheless, the language whose instrument is Aristotelian dialectic, the language of philosophy, I mean, is absolutely necessary in order that theology may become a science which merits the name.[19] All this, it seems, may be said of a philosopher *qua* philosopher: his wisdom is better than other wisdoms, because his is the wisdom which is all set to receive the wisdom of God, Who is Being. No other wisdom is in such a situation; all other wisdoms need extracurricular help, either from philosophy which issues from common sense, or from philosophy which is common sense. All this, it seems, must be said of a philosopher who philosophizes in the way described.

Is it possible to philosophize in any other way than the one described, i.e., is it possible to philosophize without discerning the cause of *esse*? Apparently it is. If we except Parmenides, who discerned the mysterious nature of that status which makes all things alike in that they are all existents, but not the equally mysterious function of being an existent, which is to differentiate all existents, if we except Parmenides, all philosophers have spoken in terms of causes. None but Christian philosophers, however, have located the cause of *esse*. The Pre-Socratics lo-

---

[19] Pope Pius XI, "Officiorum Omnium," Aug. 1, 1922, *Acta Apostolicae Sedis*, Ann. XIV, Vol. XIV, p. 455: "Etenim id quod efficit ut [theologia] vim scientiae veri nominis habeat . . . nihil est aliud quam Philosophia Scholastica, duce et magistro Aquinate . . ."

cated the cause of *esse* in a love and strife of elements. Before you smile at this, recall that this identification of a cause with love and strife is precisely the identification we make today; only, we don't name the cause "love and strife" today, nor do we allow that attraction and repulsion are causes of *esse*. Recall also that whatever you do name the cause of differentiation, you have explained differentiation perfectly, the way the Pre-Socratics explained it, if differences are only differences of shape or figure. Plato and Aristotle saw that a profounder explanation was necessary, because the differences of bodies are profounder than sensible differences. The generated and corrupted—these differ *toto coelo* from their antecedents. The son of Coriscus is not a different configuration of the atoms of Coriscus, and the dead body of either is not the living. To think that Coriscus and his son are the same, except in the different configurations of the same sort of atoms, is to think that the difference between *steak* and *Keats* is like the difference in the rearrangement of the letters of the two words.[20]

Plato thought that differences came from his Ideas. Platonic Ideas, according to Aristotle, can get nothing done —they do not have what it takes to be causes. Aristotle himself located the cause of all change in the motion of the sun along the inclined circle, i.e., in the ecliptic or zodiac circle.[21]

St. Thomas Aquinas deems that all the above explanations are concerned with the right things to be explained. For the Pre-Socratics the thing to be explained is *this* being. For Plato and Aristotle the thing to be explained is *such* a being. All these men, thinks St. Thomas, are turning about and exploring the correct problem. What keeps them from the full explanation to it, he thinks, is that they do

[20] Aristotle, *De Gen. et Corrup.*, I, 2, 315b 6-318b 16.
[21] *Ibid.* II, 10, 336a 32.

not see that we must have a cause of *being*, not merely of *this* or *such* a being. Had they seen that, they would have found in a cause of *being*, a cause also of *this* and *such* being. For, the cause of *ens* causes the causes of individuation and substance to exist, and therefore it causes individuality and substance.[22]

Christian philosophers saw that if one is to philosophize with complete competence, one must discern that the secret of the world is the fact that it exists, and that the key to that secret is the demonstration of a cause of existence. Why did they discern that secret and the key to it? Because they were told by revelation that God made the world: "In the beginning God created the heaven and earth". Whether or not, then, the world existed from eternity, at any rate and from the purely philosophical point of view, the world holds its status of being an existent from a creative cause. Upon this basis, every adumbration of this truth, every feeble expression of it, all the riches of the Egyptians were taken over by Christian philosophy. But in Christian philosophy these spoils are transformed, glorified, made new, in a philosophy which the ancients never knew, but which I'm sure, they would recognize for their very own. Who taught us the principle of causality if not Aristotle? Yet what is this principle of causality *now* if not the principle whose deepest spring is divine love? Aristotle never knew that, but can we conceive him denying it now? Can we even conceive that he would have denied it had he known the fact of creation? I am not here trying to make Aristotle say what he never said, but I am suggesting that

---

[22] St. Thomas Aquinas, *Sum. Theol.*, I, 44, 2, *resp*. For the references to Greek sources see *S. Thomae de Aquino Ordinis Praedicatorum Summa Theologiae* (Ottawa: Impensis Studii Generalis O. Pr., 1941), Vol. I, p. 280b. Cf. Aristotle, *Metaph.*, I ,3-4, 983b 6-985b 22; *Phys.*, IV, 6, 213a 29; *Metaph.*, II, 5, 1002a 8; *De Gen. et Corrup.*, II, 9, 335b 24; *Phys.*, I, 4, 187a 30; *Phys.*, I, 4, 187a 15; *De Gen. et Corrup.*, II, 9, 336a 4; *Phys.*, I, 8, 191a 27; *Metaph.*, I, 4, 985a 8; *Phys.*, I, 5, 188b 34; *Phys.*, VIII, 1, 250b 24. Cf. also St. Thomas Aquinas, *In Phys.*, I, lect. 15.

there is nothing in what he did say which prevents a Christian from saying more.

If Christian philosophy, which discerns *esse* as the heart of reality, and which succeeds in identifying the cause of *esse*, if Christian philosophy owes its existence to revelation, the question now is this: will Christian philosophy continue in existence without dependence upon the faith which created it? Since the way being is conserved is the same as the way it is created, it seems not.[23]

There is no question here of turning philosophy into theology, of arguing from dogmas to natural truths, no question of the rationality of Christian philosophy. It is rather a question of the rationality of a Christian philosopher. Revelation, according to St. Thomas, is not necessary in order to specify philosophical truth, but it is necessary for the *exercise* of philosophical wisdom. Why? Because without revelation few men, and they only at long last and with the admixture of many an error, can know natural truths about God. The Vatican Council made this principle its own.[24]

We now seem to have most of the identifiable features of a Catholic philosophy. Catholic philosophy is in the order of act, either as a habit or an operation. Between the baby and the adult there is no difference in the order of *esse*. As fully an existent as when he was a baby, an adult is not better off for having been around a longer time. Between the St. Thomas who chewed up the scrap of paper upon which was written the Angelic Salutation, an operation which his nurse tried to but couldn't prevent *(frustra adnitente nutrice)*, and the St. Thomas who had finished

---

[23] St. Thomas Aquinas, *Sum Theol.*, I, 9, 2, *resp.*
[24] St. Thomas Aquinas, *Sum Theol.*, I, 1, 1, *resp.* Cf. H. Denzinger, *Enchiridion Symbolorum, Definitionum et Declarationum de Rebus Fidei et Morum*, ed. Bannwart-Umberg, Friburgi Brisgoviae (B. Herder, 1922), n. 1786. Cf. also G. Smith, S.J., "Mr. Adler and the Order of Learning."

the *Summa,* the difference is a perfection of nature, caused, not by existing, but by a juncture of his nature to its ends. This juncture St. Thomas made freely; it was not made for him, as it is in sub-human natures. Now, the end of human nature is the good which is knowledge. To this good St. Thomas committed himself by human acts into which grace inserted itself not only so as to make those acts good *sicuti oportet,* but also so as to cause the intelligible contours of those acts, their objects, that is (St. Thomas' knowledge of entitative potency, for example, of the act which is *esse,* of the cause of *esse,* of substance whose act is *esse,* etc. etc.), to exist in an order of being which deserves no less a name than this: a new creation. Just as bread, wine, water, and oil are now new because they now savor of Christ, so also are objects of Christian philosophical wisdom new. Just as an act of bravery performed in charity is no less bravery but rather bravery more than ever, because more itself— bravery with the newness which the *esse caritatis* gives to it, so the objects of Catholic philosophical wisdom are now new with the newness which the *esse caritatis* gives to them. From even the honest intellectual or moral mistakes a man makes, as when he thinks his audacity to be bravery, or as when he thinks that effects are in their causes under wraps, something of nature is salvaged by grace. Why should we think that nothing of nature is salvaged by grace when a man's bravery *is* bravery, or when he thinks that effects in *esse* are due to the "Other" Who is *esse?* There is this difference, however, between the objects of speculative and the objects of moral knowledge. The objects of moral knowledge cannot exist except in the order of charity. There *is* no act of justice unless it exist in charity. The objects of speculative knowledge, however, can exist in an act which a sinful decision has initiated, sustained even. If one studies philosophy vaingloriously, one's philosophy may be no less true for all that. And yet, if not in charity, philosophy seems never to grow or, if in the bud, to wither there.

In point of fact, Catholic philosophy did not get into existence apart from the order of charity. Catholic philosophy got into existence by the impact of faith and revelation upon the human mind, by faith seeking an understanding of natural truths in order that faith might better understand God the Father. And just as Catholic philosophy was a new creation, so should its continuance be a continuance of that creation. If a Catholic philosopher is to continue to philosophize without the admixture in his philosophy of many an error, to philosophize from the start and not only at the end of his intellectual life, to philosophize in a numerous company of many like him, he must keep his weather-eye upon the *stella rectrix* of Catholic theology. For, if few men, at long last, and with the admixture of many an error can come to the natural truths about God without revelation,[25] it follows that with revelation, many men, right from the start of their intellectual life, and without the admixture of many an error can better come to the knowledge of natural truths about God than they could come without revelation. This in fact is what men did do.

If this be the picture of Catholic philosophy, its place in a Catholic school seems clear enough. First, it is not a waste of time, unless any and every thing is a waste of time. Secondly, its pre-eminence over all other natural wisdoms lies in its object, being, which is open in itself and in the knowledge of it to God and to the knowledge of Him. Thirdly, it must be exercised in the order of charity, because only in charity does philosophy exist as a perfection of a supernatural man and as a new creation of philosophy. And, fourthly, just as Good Friday magic changed the

[25] H. Denzinger, *op. cit.*, n. 1728.

world of philosophy from being a knowledge possessed by few men, at the end of their lives, and with large doses of error in it, so the same Good Friday magic *can* cause Catholic philosophy to continue as a knowledge possessed by many, from the moment they begin to live the life of the mind, and without many an error.

Here I feel justified in stopping, but perhaps you won't think I am justified. You may be thinking that I have not for a moment spoken to the point. The point you may say is this: What is the relation of Catholic philosophy to Catholic theology? Or this, why, if all that has been said is true, why not drop Catholic philosophy and study only Catholic theology? Or this, why make Catholic philosophy so all-fired dependent upon Catholic theology? Or this, if you do make Catholic philosophy as dependent upon theology as you do, won't theologians be moving in on us and announcing *urbi et orbi* what they think philosophy is in order that philosophy may be exactly what they think it should be if it is to serve their theological purposes?

There are two dangers: one, that Catholic philosophy be cut loose from Catholic theology. It's too late for me to make clearer my opposition to this regression of Catholic philosophy from theology. The second danger which is being signalized in all those anxious questions is this: the danger of theology swamping philosophy.

The principle which should eliminate this second danger is this: though Catholic philosophy *exists* only in Catholic theology, nevertheless it cannot exist there as theology but only as philosophy, a philosophy back from the cleaners, fresh, new, the same but renovated. Just as bravery exercised in charity cannot exist except in the order of charity, and yet it stays bravery all the same—bravery plus, so Catholic philosophy, exercised in acts of theological wisdom cannot exist except in theological acts of wisdom, and yet it remains philosophical wisdom but new withal. A philosopher does not begin by being a professional theologian, but a theologian who hopes to be a professional theologian will have to begin by being a philosopher, and both theologian and philosopher must begin by believing. At the level of their faith, a child and an adult without any profane knowledge are pretty much in the same boat: neither is a good theologian. That is why we must all try to be better theologians by understanding not only our faith but also the truths of nature which pertain to salvation. Some theologians do this very well, some do not. At any rate, no theologian can do this without some help from the sciences and particularly from the science of philosophy. True, the theologian uses all sciences for his better understanding of God the Father, but in order to use them they must exist (in charity, of course) according to their *own* scientific contours. If a theologian tries to talk about justice without knowing economics sufficiently, he talks through his hat, and if he talks about ends without knowing that the *finis qui* and the *finis cui* are inseparable facets of one end, he also talks through his hat. Not that his conclusions may not be correct—his faith minus science may be enough to make him land on his feet. But faith minus science is not enough for him, and still less for the rest of us, to land on his feet with the poise which is necessary for the *opus rationis* of a consummate theology. This being so, we should resist, it seems, the intrusion into philosophy of the theologian whose philosophy is feeble if not false. Hence to drop philosophy from the curriculum is sheer disaster for theology.

And if one says that we may keep it but should teach it in a theology class, that depends. If to teach and learn both philosophy and theology means to teach and learn both from the same textbook, the thing can very well be done if the textbook is the *Summa* of St. Thomas Aquinas. I do not know of any other textbook from which it could be done. However, one cannot well do both in the same go, even though the doing of either will always be in the same go of charity. A Christian philosopher, who must be a theologian, had better do philosophy; and a theologian, who must be a Christian philosopher, had better do theology. The principle of the division of labor seems to hold here.

The issue, however, is rather here. Can anyone but a theologian teach and learn Catholic philosophy? It seems not. This does not mean that a theologian *qua* believer—and all of us must believe in charity, is philosophically well enough equipped to talk sense, either in philosophy or theology. Besides faith, theologians need horse sense, whose refinement is philosophy, and they need other sciences as well. Now, faith will not substitute either for intelligence or for the work of intelligence. True, the *opus rationis* gets into supernature by a free decision, made in charity to do a job—like any other work. But, like any other work, it won't get into the order of charity at all if it is not there to get into the order of charity. You may decide until you are purple in the face to learn something; you won't learn anything simply under the steam of that decision. Nor will you learn anything without that decision. The vassalage of all knowledges to the kingdom of theology does not mean that they have no rights themselves. When, for example, the great St. Augustine tells us that effects are in their causes under wraps, or that the truth of our knowledge comes from God and not from things, is he respecting the rights of nature and of our knowledge of nature except in his conviction that nature truly causes and that we truly know it does? And how many are the theologians who have proposed a philosophy less acceptable than Augustine's seminal reasons and illumination? If we are to judge the competency of some contemporary theologians from their writings, there seem to be enough of them kicking around to make one suspect even those among them who ought to be above suspicion, and so the whole tribe of them might cause, unjustifiably of course, the resentment which only some of them deserve. Besides, whereas a theologian is dead right in claiming primacy for theology, it seems that some who make that claim mean by it their right to dictate the content of other fields of knowledge. They have no such right. Knowledges short of theology dictate their own content, and theologians have only the right to listen to and to avail themselves of those dictates, if and when they understand them, in order to speak better of God the Father. Should a theologian deny all this, it is small wonder that he begins to call upon God to support his position. Certainly, he cannot call upon any one else.

Lest the meaning of the statement that only a theologian can teach and learn Catholic philosophy be misunderstood, let us suppose a disagreement between a theologian and a philosopher, and let us ask under what conditions would the one be right and the other be wrong. Dismiss from your minds the illusion that a theologian is a clergyman and a philosopher a layman. States of life define neither a theologian nor a philosopher. Being a clergyman myself I rather think that we clergymen are more often wrong than layfolk, and the irritation which that statement can cause in me and other clergymen is a pretty good sign that the opinion advanced is sound. . . . To recur to our question, if the theologian is a better philosopher than the philosopher is, the theologian would be right, but only because he is a better philosopher. If the philosopher is a better philosopher than the theologian is, the philosopher would be right, but because, being a better Catholic philosopher, he is *ipso facto* a better theologian. In other words, God forbid that a theologian minus philosophy tell a Christian philosopher what to think. It does not seem necessary, however, to call upon God to avert the catastrophe of a philosopher dictating to a theologian, because God seems to have made it impossible that there be a Catholic philosopher who is not also a theologian. It seems possible, on the other hand, that there be theologians who are not particularly good philosophers. Theology transcends philosophy by as much as a theologian can be right in spite of his philosophy. A Catholic philosopher, however, is not right in spite of his theology; rather, if right, it is because of his theology. Think of the controversies *de auxiliis* and *de sacramentorum causalitate.* One party to these disputes must be wrong. Yet the Church tolerates the theology of both parties.

To conclude, we must resist, it seems, the theologian who tries to dictate what philosophy should be when he knows none, just as we must resist the philosopher who tries to tell us that in a Christian universe it makes little difference to philosophy whether or not it be exercised in the order of faith and charity.

An Instance of
Christian Philosophy

III. An Instance of Christian Philosophy

Philosophy and the Unity of Man's Ultimate End*

I

When a child obeys or disobeys a mother's injunction, e.g., not to cross the street alone, an event has intruded itself into the world which has ever confronted men with its specific mystery and wonder. I shall try to examine that mystery.

Two things can cause an examination of the mystery to fail. It will fail if we miss the specificity of the mystery. It will fail also if our examination is an idle venture from the start.

Let us first, then, briefly locate the area of the mystery. By hypothesis no harm or good will come to the mother,

* This paper was given at the 27th annual meeting of The American Catholic Philosophical Association at the University of Notre Dame, April 8, 1953. It was published in *Proceedings of The American Catholic Philosophical Association* XXVII (1953), pp. 60-83. Section II of the original paper is given in a shortened form here.

whether the child obeys or disobeys. Mother will of course feel good or bad if she ever finds out what her child did, but her feelings are not the reason for her command. By hypothesis also no harm will come to the child if he disobeys, provided only that he be very careful not to cross alone until the street is perfectly clear. Lastly and also by hypothesis no good will come to the child if he obeys and is nevertheless knocked dead by a car which comes skidding onto the sidewalk after him. Thus, no harm or good accrues to the child under the conditions stated, whether he obeys or disobeys. No harm or good! But this belies the deepest convictions of mankind! Men know that they flourish most even when their obedience brings death. *Dulce et decorum est pro patria mori.* Men know that they are wounded to the very marrow of their being by a cowardice which buys safety. "He fled full soon on the first of June, and bade the rest keep fighting." It is from our most solemn conviction that our chuckle over that line explodes, a conviction that a coward is no man to tell anyone what to do. In truth, if good and evil are equated with physical well-being and physical harm, it is quite clear that in the example given, good and evil are changing their visages under our very eyes. The specificity of the mystery now begins to appear. On the one hand, "no harm can come to the good man in this life or the next."[1] On the other hand, harm does come to the good man in this life, and the "wicked prosper," as the Psalmist complains. Here then is the question: what is the good which men choose and thrive thereon, even though their choice of it cost them their lives? Alternatively, what is the evil which men choose and mortally sicken thereat, even though they may flourish like an herb? Quickened or sickened by a food we never eat, we ask: what is this food upon

[1] Plato, *Apology*, 41; cf. *Crito*, 54.

which we mortals feed, that we are grown so great—or small?

Our examination may fail, secondly, if it is an idle task from the start to examine ourselves at those decisive moments when we make our decisions. Who cares about those intimate moments when men decide for or against the moral good? Besides, there are other moments far more revelatory of mankind than are the moments of his moral decisions, the moments when he is an artist or maker, for instance, or the moments when he is speculating about the nature of things. On two counts, therefore, it would seem that our venture of examining the mystery of human commitment is foredoomed to bring little result: to know oneself at the moments of one's commitments is an uninteresting bit of information; besides, there are bigger fish to fry: the knowledge of man's works and of man's knowledge. The mystery, in short, of human commitment doesn't appear very attractive after all, or at any rate not nearly as attractive as investigating man's works or thoughts.

"To depict himself, what a silly idea," Pascal thought of Montaigne's avowed purpose in writing his *Essais*. Silly indeed if Montaigne's self-portrait was to gull himself and his readers as a hostess' "I love your hat" may gull herself and her audience. Silly also if Montaigne's self-revelation was to reveal only Montaigne. Not at all silly, however, if a self-portrait catches the sitter at the decisive moments of his real commitments, for it is then that are revealed the greatness and misery—of what? Of Montaigne? Not at all. The greatness and misery of man, and Pascal is the first to admit it.[2] No idle venture, then, is it to examine the mysterious commitment we make of ourselves to good or evil. It is precisely here, in our choices, that we *are* our-

[2] Montaigne, *Oeuvres choisies* (Paris: Hatier, 1928), p. 35. Pascal, *Pensées*, (ed. L. Brunschvicg, Paris: Nelson, 1934), pp. 62, 64, 65.

selves, and so it is precisely here that we may know ourselves.

Should one protest that man is most himself in his arts and sciences, and that it is therefore there, in his arts and sciences, that one may learn most about him, it may be remarked that, although a man may "sack the sunset and cram it into his hold" he cannot nevertheless either set his argosy forth or bring it back safely into port ladened with booty without wishing to. Most certainly, to wish for the riches of Ormus and of Inde is not forthwith to have them. Yet the riches of the arts and sciences, and the proper use of both will not be ours without wishing to get, to know and to use them well.[3] This wish is a commitment. Thus, commitment to the venture of knowing and making things precedes, accompanies and crowns the venture itself. We shall not set sail to get them nor shall we come back safely into port with them, unless we wish to have, to keep, and to use well the treasures of knowledge. Our choices are not always attended by success, yet there is no success without choice.

Besides, to return to our starting point, the commitment itself to any venture, whatever be that venture's success in terms of value received, is the real touchstone of success or failure. Lazarus failed, on any human accounting. Yet he succeeded withal. Dives succeeded, on any human accounting. Yet his was a resounding failure. Indeed, even the commitment to an honest mistake is far better for a man than a dishonest commitment to a howling success. The good man may clumsily knock things to pieces—he

---

[3] The basic relation between intellectual and moral virtues seems to be this: the acquisition, cultivation, and good use of knowledge requires the will. Cf. St. Thomas Aquinas, *Summa Contra Gentiles*, III, 26. For further relations see *De Virtutibus in Communi*, a. VII; *Summa Theologiae*, I-II,57, 1 *resp.;* 16, 6, *resp.;* 17, 6, *resp.;* II-II, 166, 1 *resp.;* 166, 2, ad 2; 167, 2. Cf. E. Gilson, *Wisdom and Love in St. Thomas Aquinas* (Milwaukee: Marquette University Press, 1951), p. 42, note 2; p. 45, n. 5; p. 49, n. 8; p. 54, n. 22.

should be instructed and, failing instruction, prevented from doing harm, but he will not knock himself to pieces. Something is salvaged from an honest man's mistake, viz., his honesty, and this is what counts. The evil man, however, even though he may not knock other things to pieces, will most assuredly knock himself to pieces. It is his commitments which make a man good or bad, not their success, which may or may not ensue. Not that one may be disinterested in success. Far from it. Yet to have a fine house is not the same as to live well in it. This, the good life to which good men are committed and bad men are not, this remains a matter to be wondered at and examined.

II

The first feature to notice in moral commitment is this: we are already committed to loving the good which as a human good, is the *best* good there is.[4] If we name "the best good there is" an object, that object may be described as absolutely unlimited.[5] Sub-human beings also have objects even though we don't always know what those objects are nor why those objects achieve their subjects.[6] However, the object of human power is absolutely unlimited.

[4] *Sum. Theol.*, I, 18, 3, *resp.*
[5] On *intrinsic form* see *Sum. Theol.*, I, 76, 7, *resp.* On *exemplar form* see *Sum. Theol.*, I, 15, 2, *in corp.* and John of St. Thomas, *Naturalis Philosophia* (ed. Reiser, Turin: Marietti, 1930). Pars 1, q. XI, a. III, p. 240b 18; Pars I, q. XIII, a. I, p. 273b 20; Pars IV, q. II, a. III, p. 76B 40; *Ars Logica*, Pars II, p. XXI, a. IV, p. 670 sqq. On *action form* see Aristotle, *Metaphysics*, IX, 8, 1050a 23, 30; *Physics*, III, 3, 202a 13; 202b 10; *De Anima*, III, 2, 426a 9; St. Thomas, *Cont. Gent.*, II, 16; *Sum. Theol.*, I-II, 9, 30. Object form may also be an end, but even when it is, it *specifies* operation, whereas end causes the *exercise* of operation. Cf. *Sum. Theol.*, I-II, 18, 2, ad 2; *In I Sent.*, d. 1, q. 2, a. 1, ad 2. Cf. also *In lib. de Anima*, II, lect. VI, ed. Pirotta, n. 305; *Sum. Theol.*, I, 25, 1; 57, 1; 77, 3, *resp.* 82, 3; I-II, 9, 1; 18, 6; II-II, 117, 3; 153, 5; 162, 3; *De Potentia*, VII, 10; *Cont. Gent.*, I, 48; II, 98; III, 1; *Quodlibet.*, VIII, 9, 1. The best definition of *object form* seems to be in *De Caritate*, a. IV, *resp.*
[6] Aristotle, *De Anima*, II, 4, 415a 18-22: before we can state what perception or thinking or nutrition is, we must first state what each power does; then, Aristotle goes on, we must go farther and state the *objects* of those powers, e.g. food, sense-object and the intelligible. Cf. St. Thomas Aquinas, *In lib. de Anima*, II, lect. VI, ed Pirotta, nn. 305-308; *Sum. Theol.*, I, 77, 3, *resp.* Cf. also Y. Simon, *Traité du libre arbitre*

Two lines of reflection seem to establish the proposition that only a good which is and comprises all things can ever achieve human power. First, no object of human power is ever *experienced* as achieving it. Quite simply, no matter what we do there's always something else for us to do. The experience is banal. Its implication is truly stupendous. No sub-human agent is ever in our situation. Short of man no agent ever can do any better for itself than by keeping right on doing what it does. The flustered Marshal McMahon said to the Senegalese soldier whom he was decorating for bravery, "So you're the negro, eh?" "Yes, Marshal." "Well, keep it up, son, keep it up." As if the brave soldier could help it! Just so, to grow grapes—nothing better for a vine. To be eaten—the grapes might not like it, if they had feelings, but as parts of a physical whole which sustain the universe it might be that nothing better could happen to grapes than to be eaten.[7] In human agents, however, nothing here and now ever quite achieves their power. Nature, yes, something achieves nature here and now. Nature is determined to being and doing one thing.[8] One thing a sub-human structure does, one thing it is, and in being and doing that one thing it thrives perfectly. Our peculiarity lies in this: though we may thrive better by doing this rather than that, we never thrive perfectly no matter what we do. We must conclude that, because object can achieve power, either there *is* no object of human power (because no object ever achieves human power); or if there is, it is not a second-best because second-bests do not achieve power).[9] Thus we are left staring at our situation unless we open up a second line of reflection.

(Liège: Science et Lettres, 1951), pp. 39-40, n. 1; cf. Aristotle, *Nicomachean Ethics*, I, 1, 1094a 3.
[7] E. Salmon, *The Good in Existential Metaphysics* (Milwaukee: Marquette University Press, 1952), pp. 19-20. Cf. *Sum. Theol.*, I, 48, 2, ad 3.
[8] *Cont. Gent.*, II, 83.
[9] *Sum Theol.*, I-II, 2, 7-8.

The second reflection is this: human nature can be achieved only by that which is and comprises all goods, because human nature is an intellectual structure. To expand that second reflection, we may note that it is self-evident that intellectual structure anticipates its object, being. Dispute there may be about the nature of being, but no one can ever dispute that what he knows is being. Now, once it is posited that being *(ens)* is the object of intellectual structure, there is forthwith posited as the total object of intellectual structure that being which is unlimited, and thereby also that good which is unlimited. To knowing and loving the *Ipsum Esse* we are structurally committed.

We must go into this. It is a commonplace that intelligent persons are unsatisfied with surface views, accidental resemblances, shallow remarks. We say they are profound. Less figuratively, intelligent people see connections. Stupid people see no connections. To see connections, this is to discern identities. If we work this out at any level, we shall see that intelligence at any level is always busy about discerning identities.[10] Take the level of history. We see that although Socrates need not have drunk hemlock, nevertheless if he has drunk it, it is now impossible that he has not drunk it. Here intellect discerns the eternal, adamantine identity with itself of the given which need not have been given, with the given which was given.[11] Next, intellect discerns within the constellation of Socrates' predicates, such as hemlock-drinker, philosopher, friend of Plato, etc., an identical x, perhaps unknown in its proper terms, but always known as an identical "clunk" which is not a predicate but which is the subject of all predicates. Here in-

---

[10] E. Meyerson, *Identité et réalité* (Paris: Alcan, 1908), p. 365 sqq.; Y. Simon, *op. cit.*, p. 32.
[11] *Sum. Theol.*, I, 86, 3, *resp.*

tellect is discerning that essences are self-identical. Thirdly, intellect may occasionally discern in that which is self-identical the *ratio* of its self-identity, viz., its definition. For instance, "rational animal" is the identifiable factor underlying Socrates' arguments, his cooking of his food, his falling in love in and out of season, etc.[12] Fourthly, intellect discerns that self-identical essences, defined or not, are such only by "is," and if not by an "is" which is identical with *them,* then by a cause of their "is" whose own "is" *is* identical with its own essence. Throughout all these identifications, historical, perinoetic, dianoetic, metaphysical, the factor which makes them possible is *ens,* and the factor by which the unknown becomes known because it is identical with the known, that factor bears within itself, as in its womb, anything at all, even the unknown God, provided only that it be.

Perhaps the whole matter put at a different level might be more familiar. Were one of us asked why he came here, he might say that it was in order to listen to papers on philosophical subjects. And were he asked why he wished to do that, he might say that it was in order to gain philosophical knowledge. Further pressed to justify his quest for philosophical knowledge, he might grow snappish with "I have to teach this stuff." More questions would only elicit more of the same kind of answers—and more irritation. None of us likes to be pushed to reasons which are identified with the very substance of his being, because none of us knows very well the substance of his being.

One thing we do know, however, is that we are here because, all things considered, we think this is the best place for us to be here and now. Later, thank God, we shall find something better to do, but not now. What goes on

---

[12] J. Maritain, *Distinguer pour unir, ou les degrés du savoir* (Paris: Desclée de Brouwer, 1932), p. 399 sqq. Cf. Y. Simon, *op. cit.,* pp. 33-36.

here is this: we are all wishing and hoping for the best. We know perfectly well that our presence here is only a "best" here and now, not an absolute "best". Now, our wishing to know the absolute best is the structural commitment I have been analyzing. We never learned this commitment, were never taught it, cannot teach it to others. It is our endowment as intellectual structures. We are, so to say, "stuck with it," just as the vine is stuck with growing grapes. The tremendous difference between the vine's commitment and ours (i.e. the vine is stuck with a particular job; we are stuck with the best of all jobs) should not blind us to the fact that we're both stuck.

III

The necessity we are under of pursuing as good the completion of intellectual structure, which is the *verum*, up to and including the knowledge and love of God, this necessity being a structural necessity, it would seem that like all structures we must needs, barring chance, attain that object.[13] Not so. This is one more stage in our commitment.

We must commit ourselves to the exercise of our power. This is a free commitment.

Structural commitment is all on the side of formal causality, all on the side of the object. If we act, we must act because we think it good to act. We cannot act outside the framework of the good and true. They are the canvas upon which alone we may paint.[14] This is a matter of structure. But we may paint in black or white, or we needn't paint at all in a given case unless we wish to. This is a matter of free decision. To loving the good, which is the achievement of the intellect by *verum*, we are necessarily committed, but we commit ourselves freely to loving

---

[13] *Sum. Theol.*, I-II, 5, 5, obj. 1 et ad 1.
[14] J. Maritain, *Neuf leçons sur les notions premières de la philosophie morale* (Paris: Tequi, 1951), p. 83.

this instance of the good. And we can say the same thing about happiness, a transcription in terms of experience of the good: we must love to be happy, but we freely choose where we shall find happiness. So for the last end: we are necessarily committed to the last end, but not to the last end to which we *do* commit ourselves. We seek the good, or happiness, or our last end, necessarily in so far as this triad is not found in any concrete instance of them—and it is *never,* as viewed transcendentally, found in any concrete instance of them. We seek the concrete instances of this triad freely, even the concrete instance which is God. *The* good, which is and comprises all good, this we do not seek as we seek *this* good. The good we seek necessarily; *this* good, freely. Happiness, which is the totality of the good which we can enjoy, this we do not seek as we seek this concrete embodiment of our well being; we seek happiness necessarily, this concrete embodiment of well being, freely. God we do not seek as we seek our last end. No doubt He *is* our last end, but we seek Him as we seek any other concrete end, viz., freely. We stake our capital upon one horse. Our capital is our necessary love of the good, of happiness, our necessary fixation upon a last end. We freely put this money upon this or that concrete instance of the good, or happiness, or a last end. We freely decide where we shall find the happiness which we must seek; where we shall place our total good which we must desire; where the final end which must motivate all desire is to lie.[15]

Because we can, if we wish, make bad choices, pick the wrong horse (knowing of course that it *is* the wrong horse), this in a way is too bad. An agent whose liberty or power to choose can be defective is in a parlous state. At any rate the possibility of evil choices is one with the possibility of good ones. Besides, the misery of possibly de-

---

[15] Y. Simon, *op. cit.,* pp. 52-53.

fective free agents indicates their grandeur when their liberty is perfected. In heaven the freedom of the blessed will be the freedom of an act which necessarily but without coercion knows and loves God, just as God's freedom is the freedom of the divine love which necessarily and without coercion loves Himself.

To come back from the heights, we must ask at this point just how, when we freely decide to find our good, or our happiness, or our last end, in some particular instance of that triad, just how is our capital *found* in the particular instance? In other words, how shall we describe the unity of our necessary love of the good, which is consubstantial with our natures, with our free love of an instance of the good, be that instance God Himself? How does one find one's total, concrete, infinite good in a finite participation of the good?

Observe that whatever be the answer to that question, this is exactly what we do, and in so doing we are convinced that we flourish. Men choose to die for justice, and whether or not we emulate them, at any rate we applaud the greatness of their decision. They, we think, are good men, the very flower of humankind. Why do we think so? Why are they?

No doubt there is a unity by demonstration between particular goods and the good which is God. It can be proved that God exists, that He is the end of man, that between the decision to die for justice and the vision of God there is a necessary connection. Still and all, proof is not the vision of God either here or hereafter. It is not because of syllogisms that men will die. It's not in the unity of major with minor through a middle term that we find the unity of the particular with the infinite good. The unity of the infinite good with an instance of the good is a unity of love. We wish to find our total good in the particular. Obviously we do not do this without reasons, but it's not our reasons which contain God. It is our love. It is in the love act that we identify the total good with the particular. This unity is not the unity of a proof. Proved or not, the identification of the infinite analogate of the good with the finite participation of It is made by a commitment: we wish it so.

And because we wish it so, it *is* so. It is so because, were it not, the intellect could not be achieved by the *verum*, which is man's *bonum;* yet only thus can intellect be achieved. We may see the matter in this way: assume that there *is* no identity, by free commitment, of the infinite with the finite. Then it would be question only of a mistake, and anyone can make a mistake without blame. Yet a mistake *here* is a contradiction in terms precisely because it would be a willful, blameworthy mistake, i.e., an error. Anyone can bet on the wrong horse; but no one can be blamed or praised for betting on the wrong horse (we can only envy or commiserate his luck). Now precisely, we praise or blame a man for identifying or refusing to identify the good with an instance of it, because he is free to do either. Hence if a man is wrong here about the identification, or right about the lack of it, he is in culpable error which is inculpable, or in inculpable error which is culpable. A contradiction in terms either way.[16]

To find our happiness, our good, our last end, in death for justice' sake, this is not a lie, not merely because men have never thought so, but because it cannot be. Certainly we shall not *experience* our complete happiness in such a decision, nor shall we experience in it our total good or our last end. Yet we must ask whether our happiness, experienced or not, lies in our decision to identify the total with the particular; and we shall ask the question in this

[16] *Sum. Theol.*, I-II, 19, 5-6.

way. Which one is better off? The just man who suffers for justice' sake, or the evil man who suffers not at all? Ideally the just man who does *not* suffer is better off than the just man who does, or the unjust man who doesn't. And, come eternity, the just man will not suffer. Nevertheless, the just man who suffers now is flourishing in the possession of God now. He is flourishing, but not in the achievement of his sub-structures. You shall be whipped, scourged, crucified . . . (cf. *John* xvi. 2). He is flourishing in the completion of his intellectual structure.

Put it this way. We have many powers each ordered to its own good, and the good of each power is ordered to the good of the whole, viz., the intellectual structure of man. Should we pursue the object of one power so as to exclude the good of the whole to which *it* is ordered, viz., the achievement of intellectual structure, we should be pursuing an apparent good. We might rejoice over the apparent good, but only with the fictitious joy of a drunken man. We would not be really well-off with the achievement only of our sub-structures, not even as well-off as one whose sub-structures suffer for the good of the whole. What are sub-structures for if not for structure? Why do we eat except to live? Why do we live, except to know? Why do we know, except to know God? Surely one may live to eat, but that way one achieves only size. The true good for man is the achievement of his intellectual structure by knowing God.[17] That achievement is accomplished here and now by having God within our free commitment to an instance of the good.

Accomplished? Yes, but secretly, darkly, in such wise as love tokens are but an earnest and presage of love's consummation. Consider the coordinates and the curve of love. First there are the coordinates, the lovers. These are

[17] *Cont. Gent.*, I, 2.

God and man. God, the Infinite Lover, made man a lover of the good. A lover of the good begins to exist because of Infinite Love, and beginning to be because of love, he begins *in* love. This is the direction of the curve. Next man decides, not by a decision *qua* judgment, but by a decision *qua* personal commitment, to find the good which he necessarily loved from his first breath, in a good which he knows is not the best, but which he also knows is the best he can compass, the best for him here and now. Here man cannot be in error, unless we accept the hypothesis that a good man is a living lie. The curve has now taken its direction. Man begins now to be, to exist, in love. True, he doesn't possess vision; but vision is possessing him, the vision of the beloved which "is the star to every wandering bark, whose worth's unknown, although its height be taken." Vision is possessing him as the vision of the sea is possessing one who is some distance inland; there's the tang in the air, the taste in the mouth, the faint roar of the surf... These are the unseen sea, the murmurs of eternal waters. Vision is possessing him not merely as an assurance of duty well done—it's a Kantian illusion to think that doing one's duty is the sole good for man; but as to one to whom each good is the rustle of the best-beloved's garments, the touch of his hand, the breath of his face, the hair of his head.

The most mysterious aspect of this mystery is not the fact, nor the reasons, sophisticated or simple, which point to the fact. The mystery lies in our complete assurance that there *is* an identity between our total and the particular good of our own choice. Whether we succeed in thinking the matter out or not seems to make no difference. We know we are well-off only in committing ourselves to the best as we see it. As in the matter of a miracle where the wonder is not so much that miracles happen as that men believe they happen, so here: the wonder is not so much that good men stake their all upon one cast of the dice, and flourish therein—they do indeed; the wonder is their complete conviction, and ours, that they always win, i.e., the wonder is the conviction that they *have* the total in the particular. Certainly no discourse ever caused that conviction. Discourse might well teach them that such might be the case, but that there *be* such cases, such a conviction I mean, that our conviction on this point never wavers, this is a matter which only a love-act can cause, or better, this conviction is in a love act, and this act is without words. Thus it begins to appear that there is a wordless dialogue going on between God and man, a dialogue no less clear because wordless. It is even clearer. Clearer, because the language of love speaks only in love—like music, which speaks, but only in sound. Read the program of a musical concert. What futile stuff compared to the music! Just so, lovers have a language, but it is not verbal. They sit silent in each other's presence, and they know.—*Da amantem et sentit quod dico.*

I resume. Delivered over to man in man's free commitment to the good as he sees it, God resides in that commitment as an ineffable treasure. We know we have our total good in our free decision in favor of what we think best for us here and now, and we know this not just because we can prove it. We know it because our commitment is of ourselves. To stake one's very self, this in the order of operation, is to be one's very self. Should we not have our total good in that act, we would not be at all. For, to be a *good* man, this for a *free* man is to be.

IV

Now, surely the residence of God within man's free decision is more real and precious than the blood in his body. It is a taste which is not on the tongue, an odor which is not in the nostrils, a sound where nothing is heard, a vision which is seen though one's eyes be closed. In short, it is a good in which the fibers of our being exult in song, though we may feel nothing; like the good of health, only this is the health of spirit. *Expertus potest credere* . . . Yet the presage and token of the beloved's presence are not His presence. Here we are at the last stage of the mystery of our commitment.

Commitment by our structure to the good, and the further commitment by our free choices to the good as we see it, the absolutely necessary "must" of structure in *esse*, and the moral "must" of free structure in *esse*, these are the laws of nature and spirit. Spirit there cannot be unless its good be to see God. Yet there is absolutely no guarantee in nature, free or not, that man *will* see God. Faith and revelation teach us that man will see God, and that he will see God only by grace. But these, faith, revelation, grace, are so to say extra-curricular, outside the course of nature. In short, the Beatific Vision is absolutely gratuitous. It is entirely possible that the end of man might *not* have been the Beatific Vision. And if it had not been, what then?

Observe that the question does not suppose the revelation that we shall, if committed to the good, see God. On the contrary, we ask what would be the unity of man's last end if it were not known that man will see God. The answer must of course refuse to avail itself of the data of revelation.

Only two answers are possible. 1) Man, whose necessary and free structure demands vision, would have had no end, which is vision. 2) Man would have had an end, but it would not have been vision; rather, it would have been an end within nature.[18]

[18] For a bibliography and an introduction to this subject see P. J. Donnelly, S.J., "On the Development of Dogma and the Supernatural," *Theological Studies*, VIII (1947), pp. 483-491; "Discussions on the Supernat-

Each answer has its peculiar torment. The torment of the first answer is a theologian's torment; of the second, a philosopher's.[19] Theologians—I have asked the dead and many of the living ones, theologians can't quite resign themselves to a situation in which man, however felicitously circumstanced, would never see God face to face. This is as it should be, that theologians be tormented, I mean. Dogma-fired charity must needs have some of its sorrows in mystery. Philosophers can't quite see how the laws of spirit, which point to vision, can be fulfilled without vision. And this is as it should be. Philosophers must come to the point of realizing that their thinking needs grace if it is to remain good thinking.

I see no way to ease these torments. Observe, however, that even if there were a definitive answer to our question (what would have been our state had we not known that our end is the Beatific Vision?), our easement would be only intellectual. The speculative resolution of the question would have little to do with the practical situation.

Practically, all we need is the assurance of the unity of the finite with the infinite in our free acceptance of the good as we see it. This assurance is present because the union is one of friendship. All that has been said about our necessary commitment to the good, about our free commitment to the good as we see it, all this means nothing if not friendship. God causes us to love the good, which He

ural Order," *Theological Studies* IX (1948), pp. 213-249, 554-560. Cf. also A. C. Pegis, "Nature and Spirit: Some Reflections on the Problem of the End of Man," *Proceedings of The American Catholic Philosophical Association*, XXIII (1949), pp. 62-79. Vd. also pp. 47-61.

[19] Cf. Charles J. O'Neil, "St. Thomas and the Nature of Man" in *Proceedings of The American Catholic Philosophical Association*, XXV (1951), p. 46. Cf. St. Thomas Aquinas, *Cont. Gent.*, III, 48: "In quo satis apparet quantam angustiam patiebantur hinc inde eorum praeclara ingenia." St. Thomas seems to be thinking of Aristotle principally, a sort of genus of philosophers; "philosophus", he calls Aristotle. The "in quo" seems to be the necessity of finding an end for man *within* nature, and this, the philosopher knew, won't do. *Inde angustiae*. On the other hand, for a theologian theology cannot be a science without philosophy; and if there be no end, there is no philosophy.

is; and we cannot fail to love the good, which He is. He next invites us to place or find the good, which He is, in an instance of it which is either ordered to Himself or is Himself. These would be strange antics indeed on His part if He were not a friend. Now, there is no doubt that friendship is always a venture. One doesn't know what the riches are in the country of the beloved, what one is letting oneself in for in loving the other. No matter. One thing is certain: we shall always be at home with a friend. Thus, though the *sequela* of Divine friendship is not necessarily the Beatific Vision, there is this *sequela:* the complete assurance that all will be well with us. And should one persist in demanding, how *could* things be well with us without the Beatific Vision of God, or, how could things be well with us with *only* the increasing clarity of our present vision? I see no answer to such questions. And, I add, I see no practical need for an answer. Even assuming that we knew the answer, would the answer commit us to God? It would not. Our need is to commit ourselves, for this is salvation; this is to have an infinite Friend; this is the good for man so far forth as man has anything to do with the matter. Should there *be* more to the matter, should our need for God be vaster than we could ever dream, vaster than any resource within us could ever compass, what of it? What one cannot accomplish of oneself one can accomplish though one's Friend.[20] Seen from the resources of reason alone, the unity of man's last end thus seems to lie in his free commitment to whatsoever the Love which made and invites man's love wishes, for only in this commitment is man's free nature completed. We may not know what that completion is to be, but we know it will be our completion.

[20] *Sum. Theol.,* I-II, 5, 5, obj. 1 et ad 1.

The Future of Christian Philosophy

IV. The Future of Christian Philosophy

A Note on the Future of Catholic Philosophy*

Most every one of us has had the experience of being lost somewhere, say, in a forest. We were not overly anxious, for we realized that we were lost in a place, not outside it. We felt that if only we could get back to our starting point, we would not be lost there. After all, the starting point was fixed: it was there. Suppose that our starting point was not there any longer! Suppose indeed that there was no fixed starting point anywhere, on earth or in the heavens! Then we would be lost quite completely, not, to be sure, in the spot where we are—after all, we are where we are—but lost in a cosmological space.

* This paper was written for one of the volumes which had as their purpose to honor Father Henri de Lubac, S.J. It was published in French under the title, "Note sur L'Avenir de la Philosophie Catholique" in *L'Homme devant Dieu: Mélanges offerts au Père Henri de Lubac*, Vol. III (Paris: Aubier, 1963), pp. 277-285. Both the French version which appeared in that volume and the English version which appears in this book, were written by Father Smith.

It was the last conviction that Copernicus (1473-1543) and Galileo (1564-1642) planted in us. Since their day the conviction they planted has grown with our increasing awareness of the vastness of cosmological space. We know better than Copernicus and Galileo did just how badly lost we are in a space which now seems to us to be limitless.

The conviction might not have been so disturbing had it not seemed to have theological implications. If the Christian heaven was not *above* the earth, and the Christian hell *below* or inside it, just where, in the Christian world, were we? An "above" and a "below" make little sense to us who live on a planet which is but a tiny atom in a gas of galaxies, rushing, apparently at breakneck speed (or are the galaxies pulsating? Or are they a closed vortex? Or divergent explosions? A spiral? No matter.), no one knows whither or why. Thus, the total insignificance of our position in space suggested a similarly total insignificance of our position as Christians.

Our insignificance took on another dimension. Just as Copernicus and Galileo lost us in space, so *The Origin of Species* (1859) by Darwin (1809-1882) was to lose us in time, and with similar results. The *Origin of Species* quashed forever the notion that living beings were never other than as they are now. True, some species are extinct, and some will be, but every one of them came from past species, and future species will come from the present ones. The same goes for the species which is man. Of course the changes of species are not noticeable within the time span of our present observation. However, the records of paleontology, of embryology, of comparative anatomy, etc., like Galileo's telescope, enable us to see farther back into time than we can or could see without those records. Now, all those records converge upon this conclusion: man is a fiber or a filament, coming from a past of thousands of millions of years, and promising to extend into as limitless a future. A man is not a single, lone dot among many other such dots on the carpet of time. The reason is: one such dot on that time carpet cannot be interchanged with any other dot. To think that the dots are interchangeable is to think that a man could be old before he is young, that there could be a Plato before a Socrates, that the discovery of America could have anteceded the discovery of the rudder . This is nonsense. We have moved, to push the notion of evolution to its limit, we have moved from the "uncuttable," the atom, to the molecule, from the molecule to the plant, from the plant to the animal, and from the animal to our present two-legged stature, topped by a brain of stupendous complexity. We were a long time a-borning, and that long time becomes newly significant only when we realize that it is not calendar time. It is lived time. Lived time is living beings. Living beings are filaments, stretching from a past and into a future, *à porte de vue* from either direction. A full evolutionary significance, therefore, of our being here and now on earth seems to be this: our "now," and we along with it, are as insignificant as the place we are in. We are lost in time, just as we are lost in cosmological space. We are "no-when" just as we are nowhere.

Add now to the jungles of space and time[1] a third jungle, the jungle of the unconscious (Freud, 1856-1939). We are lost in that jungle too. We had thought we were most ourselves at those moments when we took ourselves by the scruff of our neck and made something of ourselves simply by deciding to. Apparently not. There is a component in our decisions which is uncontrollable by us. That component is our unconscious activity. No doubt we seem to make decisions for better or for worse, but this is definitely an illusion. We cannot control the unconscious. It con-

[1] Meriol Trevor, *The Pillar of the Cloud*, Vol. 1 (New York: Doubleday and Co. 1962), pp. 282-284. This is an excellent biography of Newman.

trols us. As for liberty, when we come to know more about that mysterious unconscious as well as the other mysterious forces which control us, our liberty will consist in an increasing ability to bottle up those forces, combine them, or get out of their way. Such manipulations will no doubt better us in many, many ways, as Marx (1818-1883) thought, and as all of us know even without Marx. Nevertheless the end of all our manipulatory antics is becoming clearer and clearer. Ancient poets described that end with beautifully poignant sadness.

Suns may set and rise again.
For us, when once our brief day has set.
There is left the sleep of one, unending night.[2]

Modern seers, through prophesying the same fate for us as did the ancient poets, are fatuous and dull in their oracles. They bid us rejoice in, and look forward to, Progress, Humanity, the Brotherhood of Man, even, God save the mark, to the American Way of Life . . . The capitalization of such and similar terms is apparently calculated to overawe and blind us to the bold fact that within a few short years none of us will be around to do any rejoicing in, or looking forward to, anything at all. The Stoics did not father such modern nonsense. They saw no bright future ahead of us where they saw no future at all.

Add a fourth and last jungle to the preceding three, and the causes of modern man's anxiety are fairly complete. This fourth jungle we were always in, and we knew it, but once upon a time man had the resource of Christian faith to confront the evil which surrounds and is in him. The

---

[2] Catullus, *Odes*, V: *Soles occidere et redire possunt. Nobis autem cum semel occidit brevis lux. Nox est perpetua, una, dormienda.* Vd. Herodotus, *History*, IX, 16: "Of all the sorrows which afflict mankind, the bitterest is this, that one should have consciousness of much, but control over nothing." And Lucretius, *De Natura Rerum*, III, 3, 972-975: ". . . see how the past ages of everlasting time, before we were born, are as nought to us. These then nature holds up to us as a mirror of the time that is to come, when we are dead and gone."

evil which surrounds him is intertwined with the good. Benignant physical forces, without consulting us, brought us into the world and keep us there for a while, flourishing with vigor and eager with the hope of youth. Then, again without consulting us, malignant forces begin to wear us out and we die. This is a complete triumph of nature over the individuals in nature. More formidable still than the evil which surrounds us is the evil which is within us, our own evil doing. "The evil that I would not, that I do," says the great St. Paul, and his words are the cry of every human heart.

The basic issue in all this begins to emerge: where shall we make our stand? Not in space. We are nowhere in space. Nor in time, for *our* time is not in our ancestry nor in our descendants. Nor in our unconscious activity, for we are not ourselves there. The question is, what identifies us? Who are we? What is our real name? Is the name of all thieves kleptomaniacs? Are the Genghis Kahns, the Adolph Hitlers, the Stalins to be named helpless victims of circumstances? Is that their real name? "Are we to substitute the psychiatrist's couch for the cell and the hangman's noose?"[3]

Our loss of identity in space, time, the unconscious, and in evil—such seem to be the components of modern man's basic and anxious question, who am I? The question has of course always been with us. Indeed, determinism vs. liberty is the "oldest chestnut in the philosophical fire."[4] Only, that chestnut is now glowing in new fires.

The answer to the question, who are we? which Catholic doctrine gives is quite well known. At any rate any at-

[3] Ved Mehta, "The Flight of the Crook-Taloned Birds—II," in *The New Yorker* (December 15, 1962), p. 129. This is an American weekly which, besides other achievements, laughs at the "right things". An admirable accomplishment. As St. Augustine remarks, "It does make a difference, what you're laughing at" *(interest unde quis rideat)*.

[4] Ved Mehta, *op. cit., loc. cit.* The question, by the way, has many other guises, e.g., is it possible to love another person without reserve, i.e., to lay down one's life for another? Is a man who suffers for justice's sake better off than the unjust man who does not? And so on.

tempt to proffer that answer here and now is inappropriate to my purpose. I wish rather to ask and to suggest a partial answer to this question: why is Catholic doctrine's answer to our question largely unaccepted if not unacceptable to the modern mind?

It simply won't do to say men refuse Catholic doctrine's answer because they are unreasonable, or because of their bad will. Nor will it do to explain all those refusals by a breakdown in communication. Breakdowns in communication will surely explain many refusals. Yet those who do accept Catholic doctrine's answer have no insuperable difficulty in understanding that answer. Communication does not fail with them.

I suggest that the answer in part is this: Catholic doctrine has two components, its philosophy and its theology. Catholic philosophy is the substructure of Catholic theology. Let us bypass here any full dress discussion of the relations between the two, and let us note simply that Catholic philosophy was written by Catholic theologians. Catholic philosophy was written by theologians in order that they and their disciples might better understand the truths of Catholic faith. Created by Catholic theologians as an answer to theological needs, Catholic philosophy since its inception has borne the mark, the imprint on it, of the theology which created it, and it has never yet lost that imprint.

This is not to say that theologians did not know the difference between their theology and their philosophy. On the contrary. They knew that difference because they taught it to us: the source of philosophy is reason; of theology, faith. Nor is it to say that a theologian's philosophy is not good philosophy. It is to say that the philosophy of theologians has been created, explained, developed and defended by—theologians. Their philosophical work seems to have on it the marks of the hands of Esau (philosophy), though their voice was the voice of Jacob (theology). Yet, upon examination not even their hands were the hands of Esau. Their hands too were the hands of Jacob, even as their voice was. And that voice which is still voicing Catholic philosophy is still the voice of Catholic theology. There is nothing bad or wrong-headed about this. Quite the contrary. Catholic philosophy is still flourishing, indeed it cannot flourish otherwise than as bespoken from the source which is the Catholic faith. The situation is simply confusing.

Confusing to non-Catholics, Christian or not, because they don't know who is doing the talking when a theologian philosophizes. Is it a theologian or a philosopher? Confusing to Catholics, because they don't know either. Is, for example, the *Summa Contra Gentiles* of St. Thomas Aquinas, "a work of purely philosophical apologetics, or is it, right from the start, even in its first (three) books, a work of theology?"[5] As is well known, Catholic authorities are divided on this issue, and if they disagree, who is to say? *Si hoc in viridi* . . . And what about the other *Summa* of St. Thomas Aquinas? How are we to identify philosophy in the *Summa Theologiae?* The question was not so urgent when philosophy had not lost its theological moorings. But it is now. Now we need some identification tabs on Catholic philosophy and it is difficult to find these tabs on a philosophy written by a theologian.

The difficulty in expounding Thomistic metaphysics is one of order. Philosophy starts with creatures and mounts up to God. Theology starts with God, and considers creatures only as related to Him. Just how then is one to write the Thomistic metaphysics which St. Thomas did *not* write?

---

[5] Henri de Lubac, S.J., *La Pensée Religieuse de Père Teilhard de Chardin*, (Paris: Aubier, 1962), pp. 94, 95 and Note 1.

How can we be sure that, beginning with creatures and mounting up to God, we are not distorting the metaphysics which St. Thomas actually did write and which began with God and considered creatures only as related to Him? The difficulty is not that St. Thomas would disapprove of inverting his own ordering of the matter. I do not think he would. The difficulty is, what would a new ordering of the matter look like?[6] I confess I don't know, never having seen it done with any decisive success. To be sure, attempts[7] are always made to write a metaphysics which starts with creatures and mounts up to God, but on the whole these attempts do not quite commend themselves to all Catholics as being philosophy. To non-Catholics these attempts do not commend themselves at all.

What to do? Apparently we need a Catholic philosophy which is not written for theological but for philosophical purposes. Obviously such a philosophy would start in faith, but it would, within the context of faith, strive to understand nature better, not the dogmas of faith. Such a philosophy would let the beacon of faith light up the dark areas of nature, just as theology does, but with a difference: a difference of thrust, of immediate interest, a difference of the sanative function of faith from faith's salvific function. It would be a work of reason healed by faith and terminating in a knowledge of nature as related to God; not a work of faith whose terminus is still faith, better understood.

How might one recognize such a philosophy? What would be the identification tabs upon it? I have already allowed that I have not yet found them. Granted this,

---

[6] Vd. the review of my *Philosophy of Being, Metaphysics I* by Armand Maurer, C.S.B. in *The Modern Schoolman*, Vol. XL (November, 1962), pp. 70-73.

[7] Vd. my *Natural Theology* (New York: The Macmillan Co., 1951) and *The Philosophy of Being: Metaphysics I* (New York: The Macmillan Co., 1961) I myself tried to do the job, but the job did not quite come off. The reviewers of those two books, though on the whole favorable and indulgent, had serious reservations to make.

granted that we can't be sure what those tabs would be until we see them, this much is certain: such a philosophy should commend itself to all because at least it exhibits a *full appreciation of all the relevant data*. The *estimate* of those data whether made by the writer or reader, would then commend itself or not, according as that estimate is truly philosophical. But first of all we must have all the relevant data.

To illustrate: *Le Phénomène Humain* of Father Teilhard de Chardin, S.J., exhibits such an appreciation of all the relevant data. One might or might not argue with his estimate of those data. One cannot deny that he proffers the data. Indeed such has been the impact of the *Phénomène* that even the scientists are being forced to see what he saw, because what he saw is there for everyone to see. This is why, I think, Teilhard de Chardin is here to stay.

By contrast, how many Catholic philosophies of man show little knowledge of evolution, of anthropology, of psychology, of the theory of myths, and so on? How many Catholic epistemologies bypass or fumble the nature of mathematical knowledge, of the knowledge of the physicist, of the creative knowledge of the artist? How many Catholic metaphysics, presumably Thomistic, so explain the subject of metaphysics, being, as to explain it away?[8] As for the Catholic philosophers of nature, they often come a bit breathless and last upon the findings of science. "Belated scholastics," I believe William James called them. Finally, how few Catholic philosophers have exploited the "experience" of God which many modern existentialists describe so well.

Despite the foregoing, the future of Catholic philosophy might not, conceivably, be too dim. If all we need for it

[8]Suarez is a case in point. Vd. his *Disputationes Metaphysicae*, Disp. XXXI, sec. 4, n. 5 in *Opera Omnia*, Vol. XXVI (Paris: Vivès, 1956-57), p.236.

are Catholic philosophers who proffer all the relevant data which experience, history, and the arts and sciences supply, and thereafter estimate those data with philosophical competence, the face of Catholic philosophy might be more easily recognizable for what it is, namely, philosophy. More recognizable to those outside the fold of Catholic Christianity, because then it would not bear upon it the identification tab of being "managed"[9] by Catholic theologians. This would eliminate the experience of confusion which the Gentiles, *sensu moderno,* suffer when confronted with the present version of Catholic philosophy. *They* see that present version of Catholic philosophy as Catholic theology, and so indeed it is inasmuch as it has been written by theologians, "managed" by theologians, so to say. More recognizable also to Catholics themselves, because they too would then see Catholic philosophy for what it can be, namely, a philosophy which is *not* managed by theologians but is managing itself. A sheer gain for philosophy all around, this new face which Catholic philosophy would then present to the world.

A new face and a more winning face as well. For that face would then exhibit lines with which Catholic philosophers and philosophers *sine addito* are already familiar: the relevant facts and a philosophical estimate of those facts. Father Teilhard de Chardin's *Le Phénomène Humain* has already broken the ground for this venture. In his *Phénomène* Father Teilhard de Chardin has so successfully scored with the Gentile world that the picture, if not his estimates[10] of it, which he presents of the human situation

---

[9] I owe this word and its meaning here to Dr. Anton C. Pegis. Cf. his Aquinas lecture, *St. Thomas and Philosophy* (Milwaukee: Marquette University Press, 1964), pp. 21, 33, 39-40.

[10] For my part, I think that Fr. Teilhard de Chardin's estimates are on the whole correct. But that is not the issue here. The issue is this: what shall we start from? From the faith, as theologians do, and with the purpose of understanding better the dogmas of faith? Or from the data of nature, with the purpose of understanding nature better in its relation to God?

is such that the Gentile world, or any other world for that matter, cannot take its eyes off the visage of man which he has drawn with such scientific rigor and such literary skill and warmth. It remains for Catholic philosophers to complete Father de Chardin's venture by estimating his findings.[11]

The theology of first rate theologians commends itself on the whole to all theologians.[12] Well? Why shouldn't the philosophy of Catholics commend itself on the whole to all philosophers, Catholics or not? I suggest, once more, that the reason why it doesn't is because, first, Catholic philosophy is not familiar to the Gentiles, written as it was by theologians. Secondly, because Catholics themselves are not yet familiar with a philosophy which is *not* identified with their theology. In other words their philosophy, which is extracted from their theology, still bears upon it the marks of the theology from which it has been extracted. And if, without the identification tab upon it of having been written by theologians, Catholic philosophy still professes to be philosophy, nonetheless it has not as yet quite found any new identification tab for itself. Were it to find that tab, then the face of Catholic philosophy would be more familiar to philosophers as such. With the familiar everyone is at home, everyone is on its side. The familiar face is a winning face. Catholic philosophy's new identification tab, to repeat, would be a philosophy, written of course by those who have the faith but for the purpose of understanding better, not the dogmas of the faith, but of understanding better creatures themselves in their relation to God. Such an understanding would then be open to the faith—for those

---

[11] The issue here is not this: have Catholic philosophers already done that job? Of course they have. The issue is rather here: has their job commended itself on the whole to the Gentile world? And if not, why not? I submit that it has not and suggest the reason for this is as described in the text: Catholic philosophy is viewed by non-Catholics as a theology.

[12] A case in point is the theologian, Fr. Henri de Lubac, S.J.

who have none. As things are now, and from the viewpoint of the Gentiles, Catholic philosophy on the whole doesn't seem to be philosophy. To the Gentiles, Catholic philosophy still looks like theology. To Catholics, Catholic philosophy, as being philosophy, is still a bone of contention.

An Appraisal of Scholastic Philosophy*

A bystander, pointing to an item on a tray of *hors d'oeuvres,* once asked me, "What is that?" "That," I answered with prompt and glib assurance, "that is a kumquat." "And what," he pursued, "what is a kumquat?" Again pointing, I said, *"That."* Here the conversation ceased not because we did not know what we were talking about, but because we had nothing further to say about a kumquat.

The situation is somewhat the same when one asks what Scholasticism is. One may indeed answer that question by saying it is the way scholastics think. One may also add a second nominal definition to "the way scholastics think" by naming the scholastics who think "the way scholastics

---

* This paper was given at the 40th annual meeting of The American Catholic Philosophical Association on April 13, 1966, at Washington, D.C. It was published in the *Proceedings of the American Catholic Philosophical Association* XL (1966), pp. 41-54.

think." This will get us nowhere, because our reaction to the first answer, namely, Scholasticism is the way scholastics think, would, I submit, be this, "oh?" And to name the scholastics who practised scholastic thinking would, I submit, elicit something like this, "oh, *them*," or possibly some scurrilous expletive. So let us try another tack.

Doctor Julius Weinberg, Vilas Professor of Philosophy at the University of Wisconsin, after an excellent lecture he gave us at Marquette in 1964 on William of Ockham, made an off-the-record remark which may serve as a preliminary description of Scholasticism. "I like to read the scholastics," he said, "because they always try to make sense." So indeed they do, even should they make little sense to us, quite as they often made little sense to one another.

And what—this is the crucial question, what were the scholastics trying to make sense out of? They were trying to make sense out of their faith in the Word of God. It is no longer possible to question that answer and its implications. Drawn from dozens of Gilson's books and hundreds of his articles, that answer and its implications is the very heart of Gilson's thought.[1] The starting point, then, of the scholastics' thinking was their faith.

An accessible and unquestioned source of their faith was Holy Scripture. But, unlike the eunuch who could make no sense out of Isaias until the Apostle Philip made it for him (*Acts* viii. 27-35), the scholastics had no Philip around to tell *them* what Scripture meant. So, in order to find out what Scripture meant they went to the Fathers.

---

[1] *A Gilson Reader, Selected Writing of Etienne Gilson,* edited with an introduction by Anton C. Pegis (New York: Doubleday and Co., 1957), pp. 159-166. The title of the selection is "Historical Research and the Future of Scholasticism;" it is also found in *The Modern Schoolman,* XXII (1951), 1-10; also in *Scholastica ratione historico-critica instauranda* (Rome: 1951), pp. 142, et sqq., under the title "Les recherches historiques et l'avenir de la Scholastique." Paradoxically one might say that *A Gilson Reader* is probably the best book Gilson ever wrote.

Where they got stuck over the sense which the Fathers made of Scripture, they thumbed the Commentaries and the Sentences. When Commentaries and Sentences failed them, they went to the *Summas* of the theologians. Lastly, theologians failing them, they addressed themselves to the philosophers in order to find out what the theologians meant.[2]

The philosophers from whom the scholastics took the conn were of course Plato and Aristotle, and indeed it is even now impossible not to take a long, hard look at the courses plotted by those two superb navigators of the seas of thought. Nor would anyone care or dare to do so. The history of philosophy is indeed "a series of footnotes," beginning with Aristotle's "to Plato."[3] Nevertheless, though the scholastics took the conn from Plato and Aristotle, they laid and followed a different course. They had to. Neither Plato's Ideas nor Aristotle's forms satisfied the demands of Christian theology. Scholastics had learned from revelation another path, a path which, starting from faith, led through a theology to a philosophy within that faith. The heart and center of that philosophy was a metaphysics which "maximized the most basic notion of all: namely, the notion of God as a pure act of being."[4] Such a maximum is not to be found in Plato's Ideas nor in Aristotle's forms, neither in the forms of matter nor in the subsistent forms which are separated from matter and are substances.[5]

[2] *Op cit.*, p. 159, Hereafter *op. cit.* will always indicate *A Gilson Reader*.
[3] Quoted from Alfred N. Whitehead by Arthur O. Lovejoy in his *The Great Chain of Being, A Study of the History of an Idea* (The William James Lectures delivered at Harvard University, 1933) (Cambridge: Harvard University Press, 1936), p. 24.
[4] *Op cit., Introduction*, p. 15. *Vd. op. cit.*, p. 63, the title of the selection is "The Distinctiveness of the Philosophic Order;" also in *Philosophy and History*, ed. R. Klibansky (Oxford: University Press, 1936), pp. 61-76. English translation is by D. A. Patton. *Vd.* also *op. cit.*, "God and Christian Philosophy," pp. 203-206; also in *God and Philosophy* (New Haven: Yale University Press, 1941), pp. 38-73.
[5] *Op. cit.*, pp. 142-148. The title of the selection is "Theology and the Unity of Knowledge;" also in *The Unity of Knowledge*, ed. L. Leary (New York: Doubleday, 1956), pp. 34-36.

If that maximum cannot be found in Plato or Aristotle, it is safe to conclude that it cannot be found in Greek philosophy at all, not even in its most faithful adherents, the Platonists and the Arabs. If, then, Greek philosophy came into Scholasticism, and it most certainly did, it did not stay Greek in Scholasticism—like a recognizable, because undigested, lump in a gastric system, or like a diluted mixture of wine and water. Rather, Greek philosophy was changed, as was the water at Cana, into "the wine of Christian theology."[6] The names of that new wine, Christian theology, Christian philosophy, *sacra doctrina,* are less important than what they named. They are all names for theology. Like all wines, some theologies were good, some not. The good wines quite satisfied the demands of Christian theology; the "no-goods" more or less failed to. As with all good wines one always seems to be the best of all. If one has not enough good taste to recognize the best wine, one may get some extrinsic aid to help his choice from the *Aeterni Patris* of Leo XIII. In the *Aeterni Patris* Leo speaks of St. Thomas Aquinas as "the chief and master of all scholastic Doctors."[7]

Many other Doctors of the Church, Scholastic and non-scholastic proffered a theology quite adequate to their faith, not indeed because St. Thomas' "pure act of being" excluded *their* maximization of that most basic notion of all philosophy, but because their maximization was reached from different launching pads.

St. Augustine, for example, started from his experience of God in an act of faith. To paraphrase that experience, it was his "I believe, therefore I am." Augustine's *Credo* had lines of communication with matter, the matter of a be-

[6] *Op cit.*, p. 294. The title of the selection is "St. Thomas and Our Colleagues;" also given as an Aquinas Lecture at the Aquinas Foundation at Princeton University, March 7, 1953. The "water into wine" text is in St. Thomas Aquinas, *In Boethii de Trinitate*, II, 3, *ad* 5.

[7] *Aeterni Patris*, August 14, 1878, in *The Church Speaks to the Modern World; The Social Teachings of Leo XIII* (New York: Doubleday, 1964), p. 43, [17].

lieving man desperately struggling to win an enfleshed salvation, a salvation which was assured in principle at the moment when Augustine freely believed in these words: "I have overcome the world . . . You believe in the Father, believe also in me." Speaking philosophically, one might say that Augustine's *credo* was a principle of induction not a Cartesian principle of deduction. As good a man as any normal Christian, Descartes knew he could not syllogize his way into heaven. Yet he tried to syllogize his way to the existence of God the Creator by thinking simply of thinking. St. Augustine did not. He knew that just thinking was no guarantee of thinking well, still less was it a guarantee of living well. For Augustine some factor had to take charge of or manage his thinking, and, so managed, Augustine would attain the best possible sort of thinking and living. The managing factor of his thinking was his faith—*nisi credideritis non intelligetis;* the result of such management was an answer to his hope, *noverim Te, noverim me.*[8]

Saints Bernard and Bonaventure continued the Augustinian tradition by putting to the fore the ecstatic and mystical elements of Augustine's *credo*, and by exploiting those elements to their fullest expression, even at levels where mysticism is only in germ, e.g., at the level of "lending books."[9] (St. Bonaventure's advice on the business of lending books amounts to this: if you are afraid that the borrower will broadcast the content of a book before you do, and so you won't have anything to say when you are asked what is in the book—by all means lend it; the font of God's wisdom and love will not run dry just because it has run dry

---

[8] *Op. cit.*, pp. 75, 76 94-96. The titles of the selections are "The Idea of Philosophy in St. Augustine and St. Thomas;" "The Future of Augustinian Metaphysics," also in *A Monument to St. Augustine*, (London: Sheed and Ward, 1930), pp. 278-315. The *nisi credideritis* . . . is from St. Augustine's *De Libero Arbitrio*, ch. 2, n. 6 (PL 32, col. 1243).
[9] St. Bonaventure, *Determinationes quaestionum*, II, 21; *Opera Omnia* (Quarrachi), Vol. VIII, pp. 371-372.

in you). Only he who is prepared to deny the continuity of the grace of baptism with the grace of the Beatific Vision can fail to see the rich and permanent capital in such and like commentaries which these two Saints have made upon even our most lowly experiences of God.[10]

Henry of Ghent maximized the notion of God as a positive perfection, not just a negative counterpart of a finite perfection. Clearly, Henry's point was well taken, but his maneuver wound up in a "negative" theology, not in a theology *by* negation. A theology by negation will indeed deny finite perfections to God, but it will leave us still staring in wonder at an act of being which absorbs all perfections into itself. In other words, in a theology by negation whatever you can say of God *is* his being. In a negative theology God's being is whatever you can say of it, provided you straightway unsay what you have said of it. Both theologies leave us staring in wonder at God, but in a theology by negation there is still left some feature to stare at, the feature, namely, of existential act; in a negative theology we seem to be stranded before a completely unknown, because denied, perfection of God. In sum, in a theology by negation God is a feature we already know, viz., existential act, and the knowing of that feature is always God's grip or squeeze upon our intellects even before that squeeze causes the conclusion, God exists, to pop out. In a negative theology the analogue, existential act, is admittedly absent.[11]

For Scotus, the concept of being *(esse)* was a univocal, gripped either by the mode of infinity or the mode of finitude. Very well. The issue, though, is not precisely there.

---

[10] *Op. cit.*, pp. 118-122. The title of the selection is "The Spirit of St. Bonaventure;" also in *The Philosophy of St. Bonaventure,* tr. Dom I. Trethowan and F. J. Sheed (New York: Sheed and Ward, 1938), pp. 470-495.

[11] *Op. cit.*, pp. 148-149. The title of the selection is "Theology and the Unity of Knowledge;" also in *The Unity of Knowledge,* ed. L. Leary (New York: Doubleday, 1956), pp. 35-46.

No doubt either mode can be conceived as grabbing hold of a univocal factor, but not unless there exists an infinite mode of being (that there exists the finite mode of being needs no investigation). So Scotus, excellent philosopher that he is, proves the existence of an infinite mode of being in the following way. Being is either produced or unproduced. Since a produced being is not *possible* without an unproduced being, an unproduced being is *possible*. Moreover a possible unproduced being must exist, else it would not be possible, and it has been shown to be possible. Finally, an existing unproduced being cannot be limited upon the score that it produces, and so it exists and it is infinite.[12] All this is excellent thinking—such an exquisite march of perfect syllogisms! Surely anyone can live in that intellectual climate provided that being be univocal. All we need to traverse Scotus' path is a long deep breath between each stepping stone of his proof, confident that between each stone there is beneath, the hard, continuous support of a univocal. For many, that in-between support, like water, cannot be walked upon.

It is not possible on this occasion to fill in the history of Scholasticism from the 17th to the early part of the 20th century. Suffice it to say that the metaphysics which maximized the notion of the pure act of being or at least had in mind a genuine, if dialectic, maximization of infinite perfection, gradually became detached from the theology which inspired it. So detached, scholastic philosophy was like a fish lifted from the theological water which was its life. Naturally the fish died, and pretty soon there lingered about that dead fish only the worsening odor of what it

[12] *Op. cit.*, pp. 127-140. The title of the selection is "John Duns Scotus;" also in *The History of Philosophy in the Middle Ages* (New York: Random House, 1946), pp. 454-64. See *op. cit.*, p. 140, n. 1, for an indication of the sources in Scotus for his position.

once was. It stank. If the figure seems too strong, let us say that it "withered and died."[13]

Whenever scholastic philosophy worsened, the theology from which it was lifted became brackish water, drinkable but no longer quite sweet. For, "if theology is the understanding of the faith, we cannot isolate that understanding from the faith whose understanding it gives; nor can we isolate faith from the understanding which it is seeking."[14] To restore, then, Scholasticism to itself we must, first, "listen to the counsel of history: scholastic philosophy must return to theology!"[15] Secondly, we cannot, history shows, "we cannot isolate faith from the understanding it is seeking," not without damage to theology and the philosophy within it. These counsels are the more urgent because "Scholasticism, covered over by more than five centuries of dust, is now experiencing its greatest evil—the ignorance of its nature."[16]

Gilson made that remark in 1951. He would not, I think, make it without qualification now in 1966. Things are much, much better now. From the late twenties Scholasticism has recovered, along with the proper maximization of the notion of the pure act of being, its counterpart, viz., the maximization of the notion of human nature. Human nature is better known now as being open to return by its knowledge and love into the God from Whom it issued. From the middle 40's that openness of human nature has been further spelled out for us as meaning a nature whose sole end is to be by grace what the Second Person is by nature, a son of

---

[13] *Op. cit.*, pp. 49-63. The title of the selection is "The Distinctiveness of the Philosophic Order;" also in *Philosophy and History*, ed. R. Klibansky (Oxford: University Press, 1936), pp. 61-76. The English translation is by D. A. Patton.
[14] *Op. cit.*, p. 162. The title of the selection is "Historical Research and the Future of Scholaticism." *Vd.* above, n. 1.
[15] *Op. cit.*, p. 165.
[16] *Ibid.*

God. Gilson did the first job; Henri de Lubac, S.J., among other things, did the second.[17]

It is not astonishing that both maximizations proceed *pari passu.* If one is missed, so also will the other be missed. And one or the other has more than occasionally been missed. Pelagianism was an heretical miss. Pelagianism held that human nature has resources within itself to reach the Beatific Vision. On the other hand, to say that the resources which human nature *has* are sufficient to set it up in business here and now, and perhaps *per omnia saecula saeculorum,* as fully equipped as any other nature to reach an end *in* nature, this is surely bad philosophy which will somehow taint Christian theology. For, such a nature is a reviviscence of an Aristotelian nature within a Christian world. It won't work. It never did work. Christian theology from the very beginning barred the door to the notion of an Aristotelian nature, and one might well question the tactic of admitting by the back door a nature whose entry had been barred by the front door. It is high time that this funny business of cross-breeding a Christian with a pagan nature should stop.

In principle such hanky panky has been stopped. We have only to exploit now the findings of Gilson and de Lubac, to keep well tracked on the maximization of the pure act of being and its counterpart, the maximization of an intellectual nature which, issuing from divine love, can only return into that love or else remain as forever restless as it is now, with no end in nature, nor (when its genuine end has been refused) with any end at all. "Thou has made us for yourself, Lord, and our heart is restless till it rest in Thee."[18]

[17] Henri de Lubac, S.J., *Surnaturel* (Paris: Aubier, 1946); *Le Mystère du Surnaturel* (Paris: Aubier, 1964). De Lubac puts Gilson's remark about Scholasticism's ignorance of its own nature at the very head of his second book on the question, no doubt because it is one of the inspirations of his own remarkable second book.
[18] St. Augustine, *Confessions,* I, 1 (PL 32, col. 661).

The lines which such maximizations will take will not change their direction. The stance which Scholasticism at its best has always taken on the end of man will always stay the same. Scholasticism today need only take a long, hard look at all sorts of new findings in psychology, anthropology, sociology, physics, political and social studies, etc., etc. Nor will that long, hard look discover items in the field of science to which Scholasticism would have to adapt its theology and philosophy. Should scholastics try that tack, they would have to change their faith in God's word even as scientists keep changing their acceptance of science's word. This scientists have done all the way from Ptolemy through Copernicus, Galileo, Newton, Einstein, Planck, up to and including the word which is the "solid state" theory, or its alternative, the "big bang" theory.

The solid state theory describes a future as far ahead of us as we are ahead of the Renaissance.[19] We are ahead, far ahead, of the Renaissance in travel, communication, tools, —in science in short. Our future state cannot be along our curve from the Renaissance to us. Somewhere soon that curve must level off, flatten out, like a child's growth. Children don't keep on growing after manhood. At manhood growing stops. Then the genuine accomplishments of manhood begin. Just so, a world unified by travel, communication, and mutual danger must level off at the top as does an S or logistic curve. To acknowledge the bending over or flattening of the top of the logistic S curve is simply to acknowledge physical, natural, economic *limits* to everything; it is not quite the same as to acknowledge a *slowing up* of the intellectual returns or dividends of science. Those limits are "steady-state" forms which can accommodate further technical developments without a great deal of additional structuring of, or in, the curve itself.

[19] For the solid state theory's exposition I am indebted to John R. Platt's article in *Science*, CXLIX (1965), 607-13.

If, now, we ask for examples of what those solid states promise to be, the answer seems to be the following. We level off at being able to deliver 50 billions of electric volts, because there is not enough money and human effort to deliver more. We also level off in our expenditures for sociological research, at least in the United States, because we cannot afford much more than 3% of our national income, and we are close to that 3% plus now. We level off also when the information which our computers supply can travel between their parts with the speed of light. We level off in automation when we solve the problem about what to do with the leisure which automation will allow us. We level off in communications when sight and sound can be transmitted around the world in two seconds; that leveling will be the provision of more networks to disseminate the same information. The speed of travel too will level off at the speed of getting into, or coming back from, orbit, or by staying at home. We shall level off also in space if only because we can't inhabit *all* the galaxies.

There is more. Our increase of life expectancy and the decrease in the death rate are "spurious" as long as nuclear danger is uncontrollable, so spurious that one may say "never have men had such a slim chance of survival." This leveling off is a constant state of fear for the next ten to twenty years during which our chance of survival is fifty-fifty. And even if *that* fear disappears, there is this one: within an uncertainty of fifty years or so, the time when population growth slows up or levels off from starvation is only two long lifetimes, no greater than the age of the United States. Lastly, there is the leveling off by our personal death.

If there is to be no survival after death, there is no point in surviving here and now, whether we speak of personal survival or the survival of our descendants. To remind

Christians of this is fatuous, I know. But to remind those who read our future as a Utopia or as an idol worship of Progress, Humanitarianism, Struggle, Power, or any similar bit of capitalized nonsense does not seem fatuous if only for the reason that we shan't be around to enjoy a Utopia; and even if we were, our struggle, as Camus so well saw, would still be as Sisyphean as it is now. It is the alternative of our complete survival as opposed to complete destruction by violence or a natural death that Christianity proposes to everyone.

There is no need to argue the merits of that proposal now. It will suffice to know *how* that proposal is made by Christianity. It comes as a package deal. The items of that package deal are faith, theology, and a philosophy.

Let us focus on the last item, philosophy. There is no absolute necessity that a philosophy of Christian theology be scholastic philosophy. The Fathers had none. There is need, though, that the philosophy of Christian theology be a metaphysics, whether scholastic or not. Nor can that metaphysics be based upon the contributions of science. No first rate theologian ever launched his theology from that pad. True, a theologian must lop off from the findings of science whatever does not help to illumine the pure act of being, and retain the findings which do. If he did not, his philosophy would be Plato's, or Aristotle's, or Averroes', or Avicenna's, or Descartes', Kant's, Hegel's, Heidegger's, or some other present version of those named. So to lop off presupposes of course that a theologian knows what to take and what to leave. If he does not, that is too bad. His theology will suffer even as his philosophy would be a nonphilosophy of Christian theology. It is a losing fight to oppose the latest scientific versions of matter which scientists give. Each new version will purify itself and all the better for it if theologians do not interfere.

Since theology must have a philosophy, the question is pertinent, what philosophy? Certainly, as was said, it is not of absolute necessity that it be scholastic philosophy. The Fathers were not scholastics. Nor will it do to say that any old philosophy will suffice for Christian theology, certainly not the philosophy of Plato's Ideas or Aristotle's forms, or the derivatives therefrom; and when a Christian rejects, not Plato but Plato's Ideas, not Aristotle but Aristotle's forms, one has pretty well covered in principle the field of a non-Christian philosophy. The best possible philosophy for a Christian is the one "to which is united obedience to the faith," and that philosophy is St. Thomas Aquinas'.[20] That St. Thomas should happen to be the best Christian philosopher is a matter of history. That his philosophy should be the best philosophy is not.

This is not to say that Thomism is our only port in the storm of a rapidly congealing or solidifying state of human nature, whether that state be solidified into a future Utopia (which we shall not be around to enjoy) or into a permanent state of natural death or death by violence. Thomism is the name for the philosophy of those who either profess to follow St. Thomas' guide lines and do, or those who simply profess to follow those guide lines. There is a difference. St. Thomas is not the first and last Thomist, no more than St. Ignatius is the first and last Jesuit, (I am more tempted at times to assert the second proposition rather than the first.) I shall not name here those unauthentic Thomists (or Jesuits).

Those genuine Thomists—there is a feature about the discourse of many of them which seems a bit distasteful to the modern mind. Negatively, that feature seems to be a lack of eloquence; positively, it is a rather constant use of dialectic as an instrument.

[20] Leo XIII, *op. cit.*, p. 38.

The characteristics of dialectic discourse seem to be breadth, clarity, comprehensiveness. A dialectic mind is robust, complete, confident. It does not progress by stages as one claws his way up a mountain. It is on the mountain top to start with and from there details the scene beneath. It does not conquer as it goes; it has conquered once for all and then proceeds to skirmish in rear guard actions. Quick to answer, it satisfies us with its vigor, inspires us with the sweep of its *summas*, makes us confident that issues seemingly unsolved at the first go will be seen later to have been solved at the very start. For example, a dialectic discourse may begin with the question "does God exist?" Then it will say "it seems not," adducing the reasons why it seems not; then it will move to an "on the other hand it seems so," adding the reasons why it seems so; lastly it will mop the pieces by refuting the arguments in favor of the "it seems not." Such discourse does not sit easily with us now, not even when it is cast into the thesis form with its adversaries named, its *probo,* its objections and answers to them.

Nowadays we prefer thinkers who are as deep as they are broad, as exact as they are full, ones who grip a subject rather than bestride or enfold it, ones who are forever climbing rather than looking back over ground gained. Such minds proceed by a slow assimilative progress, like an amoeba, advancing by indirection, turning an obstacle here, assimilating it there, or sweeping it along with itself, or simply leaving untouched what it cannot, at present, take in. Such minds will arrive if given time, as a drop of oil will eventually stain a whole batch of linen. They will rarely pitch camp and sing of victory. They are too busy enlarging by tooth and nail their little *pied-à-terre.* They will never say "I always tell 'em." They never completely win; they are always winning. Slow to answer, their answers dissatisfy themselves more than their questioners.

Like Chesterton's men, they have "wars they hardly win and souls they hardly save." They write slowly, painfully, are better critics than creators, more likely to muddle through than strike well planned, decisive blows, and are silent under criticism.

The distinction between the two types may seem overlapping as Dr. Johnson's division of the Scotch, "Scotchmen and damned Scotchmen," and in a way it is. We never meet pure instances of either type. Each style borrows from the other. There are various combinations of the strength of Richard's sword and the keenness of Saladin's scimitar. It is not a question of dividing types according to the doctrine professed by them. It is rather a question of recognizing two different ways of professing a doctrine, two different, though mingling and criss-crossing ways of coming to the truth. Newman, e.g., scatters lightly over his pages the nice distinctions which the dialectic mind puts into the thesis itself. Unlike Newman's *Idea of a University* a scholastic discourse on education would probably start with an analysis of the human act; so too a scholastic discourse on the nature of history would likely begin by examining the *necessitas antecedentis* and the *necessitas consequentis*;[21] and of course a scholastic would take on Plato with the famous *id quod* and *modum quo* distinction. All this scholastic discourse is very well, but it can turn sour as it did with the scholastic who would rather define compunction than have it. On the other hand, a humanist may turn sour too: unable to define compunction, he may be unable to distinguish between compunction and the thrill attendant upon the rapid descent of an express elevator.

[21] Mircea Eliade in his *Le Chamanisme et les techniques archaïques de l'extase* (Paris: Payot, 1951), p. 239, fn., has a much better starting point for distinguishing history from science: "It is not quite clear why the fact that the discovery of geometry was due to the empirical necessities of irrigating the Nile delta, can have the slightest importance in validating or invalidating those laws." (My translation.)

Recall the less fantastic instance of those who concluded by a sort of inverse ratio that since God is infinitely good, we must be infinitely rotten.

We must have both types of discourse, the humanist's and the dialectician's: the humanist's if we are to have historians, more faithful to fact than to clarity; if we are to have philosophers who can inspire a sense of awe before mysteries not dreamt of in philosophy; if we are to have theologians who do not so explain as to explain away (e.g., a Person of the Trinity is a relation; a relation is an *ens minimum!*); if we are to have novelists who can strike a chord to which we vibrate; if we are to have scientists who "in nature's infinite book of secrecy can a little read." All these reflect more fully than does the dialectician, life's turbulence and mystery. Yet the dialectician is more understanding, more calm, more steady at the fixed points about which he turns. He gives better advice. From him we learn by listening. With him life is less an adventure than a lesson. Though he "never saw a moor" or the sea, yet knows he how "heather looks and what a wave must be;" though he "never spoke with God, nor visited in heaven; yet certain is he of the spot as if the chart were given."[22]

Yet there seems to be more to this matter than a difference between two types of discourse about the same things, dialectic type and the humanistic type, scholastic discourse and non-scholastic discourse, between St. Thomas' intellectualism and St. Augustine's voluntarism. At their peaks any type of discourse gets into existence for the same reason, viz., because it exists. So too does any task, for example, changing tires, mixing a drink, building cities, speculative thinking and practical. The point is, any task may very well be described, but that description will fit no existent thing unless that thing exists.

[22] *The Poems of Emily Dickinson,* ed. Thomas H. Johnson (Cambridge, Mass.: Harvard University Press, 1958), Vol. II, p. 742.

We have come to the crucial and the only point to which I have been headed all along. Let us name any task from the viewpoint of its achievement, keeping in mind (1) that we wish a name for that achievement which will name it before that achievement exists, and (2) which will also name that achievement without specifying, by the name, what that achievement is. That name is "object."[23] And since "an object has, in a way, the aspect of a form," let us further name that object a "formal object."[24] Here, in their formal objects lies the difference between philosophy and theology. Philosophy's formal object is anything in its relation to God. No philosopher ever omitted God from his discourse except by deifying a false god. A philosopher simply must talk about God or a god. Theology's formal object is God (not in relation to things, He has no such relation), the Creator, Redeemer, and Sanctifier of the world —the revealed God. With this distinction many scholastics think to have a perfect distinction between the two disciplines of philosophy and theology. If the validity of that distinction of theirs is questioned they may begin to breathe heavily, investing their words with sacral solemnity, and may succeed in overawing the uninitiated. I rather think that such a distinction between philosophy and theology is valid only up to a point, and for the following reason. Formal objects do not exist unless—*mirabile dictu!* they exist. And exist they do not except (1) when they are achieved (and then they are not named formal objects at all; they are informed beings), or (2) except when they exist in their being-known and their being-loved *esse*, the *esse*, in other words, of their intentionality. To philosophize about formal objects as if they were separated, in the very

---

[23] St. Thomas Aquinas, *De Caritate*, IV, *resp.:* "... potentia hoc ipsum quod est, dicitur in ordine ad possibile, quod est objectum." Vd. *De Veritate*, XXI, 1 resp.
[24] St. Thomas Aquinas, *Sum. Theol.*, I-II, 18, 2, *ad* 2.

philosophizing about them, from the philosophizing *esse* (intentionality) by which they exist, this is sterilized philosophizing.

If, now, one asks what that "philosophizing" *esse* is—that depends. The philosophizing *esse* of a Greek philosophy is—a Greek's philosophizing; and so for any philosophizing *esse:* it is the philosophizing *esse* of the philosopher concerned. The Christian's philosophizing *esse* is that (1) of a believer in God's word, and (2) that of one who has some understanding of God's word (a theologian). And now it may be asked, won't the uniting of philosophy to theology destroy a distinction already established by the genuine distinction of their formal objects? I should say, no, it won't. It will destroy, though, the notion that a Christian's philosophical thinking is separated from, is not also, his theological thinking. We must keep in mind that though habits are specified by their formal objects, nonetheless they do not exist in a Christian except in his believing and his theologizing. And it is as so existing that we must "pronounce upon them."[25] That "pronouncement," so far as it concerns St. Thomas' philosophy, has been adequately made by Jacques Maritain. The epithet "Thomistic philosophy," he says, would no doubt have displeased St. Thomas very much; it is not fitting to stamp a philosophical doctrine with the name of a theologian; nor is it fitting to name with the name of any man a philosophy which ought to renew itself from generation to generation and from age to age, and to nourish itself on the whole past in order constantly to transcend it. If we do excerpt from St. Thomas his philosophy, withdraw it from the light of its theology,

---

[25] St. Thomas Aquinas, *De Caritate*, III, *resp.:* ". . . de habitibus oportet nos secundum actus judicare."

we have a product which is neither philosophical nor theological; it is a lifeless theology passing as a philosophy.²⁶

A final remark and a comment. There is much talk these days about "relevance," "updating," "existentialism," "the new theology," "the situation," etc. One can be fairly certain that when St. Thomas is the topic of discourse, those words are meant to describe his work in reverse: his theology is out of date, irrelevant, his situation is not ours, his philosophy is a pyramid. Admirable in a way, but as useless as Cheops' tomb.

"Who is to make our contemporaries aware of that taste for being, that profound and indescribable love of being, that glowing enthusiasm, that sober tenderness, strong, all but infinite, for humanity, which breathes from every page of the Angelic Doctor? Who is to make them aware that beneath the limpid, clear, concise formulas, stuffed with meaning, there pulsates a passionate enthusiasm for "the splendor of human nature"? *Pulsates* is ill said. We need a word here which would mean the uttermost intensity of love without suggesting its disquiet, precipitation, anxiety. It is the fullness of that love which hides its vivacity from inattentive eyes. We are tempted to judge St. Thomas bloodless and abstract. But that impression vanishes in the measure that we grow familiar with him. The simplest, most usual expressions light up in the totality of his thought, and open up intelligible perspectives which are infinite. The same can be said for the all embracing principles, so often found in St. Thomas, which seem empty to the superficial and meaningless to the inattentive, but which are seen to fill themselves with concrete reality to the extent that they are better understood. For example, 'those who wage war are trying thereby to arrive at some sort of peace,—the safety of

---

²⁶ Jacques Maritain, *La philosophie morale* (Paris: Gallimard, 1960), pp. 8-9. *Vd.* Anton C. Pegis, "Sub Ratione Dei," in *The New Scholasticism*, XXXIX (1965), 141-157.

the multitude is preferable to the peace of any number whatsoever of individual men,—a man is bound by a sort of natural fittingness to live pleasantly with others'. The *Summa*, seen from far off, looks like an arid desert, but one who enters it, sees there flowing in full flood 'the milk of human kindness'. The shouts and excessive gesticulations of the philosophers of insubordination, the noisy lovers of humanity in revolt, how cold they leave us, compared to that great love of the human race which is consubstantial with reason itself! What intellectual misery is revealed in the very excess of their exclamations! The candid voice of St. Thomas is stronger. This or that word of his penetrates to the depth of the heart without our noticing it; in time, we find that it has caused there a deep and delightful wound, and has melted our heart with glowing and tender love for humanity. The old prophet said 'don't despise your flesh'. It is the same lesson which issues, with irresistible persuasiveness, from St. Thomas' lips; and it is surely not of him that one could say, as of Plotinus: 'he hated to be a man.' Whatever is human he loved, enjoyed, understood, made his own. But this was because his intelligence was entirely freed from particular passions, because he was sympathetic to the whole of reality, because his candor was infinite, and because his taste for being was without limits."[27]

If those beautiful and true words of Father Rousselot's about St. Thomas Aquinas are taken lightly by anyone, one can only conclude that such a one has not read St. Thomas.

---

[27] Pierre Rousselot, S.J., "L'Esprit de St. Thomas" (*à propos* of R.P.A. Sertillanges' *St. Thomas d'Aquin*), *Etudes*, CXXVIII (1911), 626-28; also in Rousselot's *L'Intellectualisme de St. Thomas* (Paris: Beauchesne, 1924), "notice sur l'auteur," pp. ix-xi. (My translation.)

BL BR
51 100
.S573 .S53